cherished

cherished

21 Writers on Animals
They Have LOVED and LOST

Edited by Barbara Abercrombie

New World Library
Novato, California

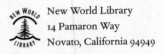 New World Library
14 Pamaron Way
Novato, California 94949

Text design by Tona Pearce Myers

Library of Congress Cataloging-in-Publication Data
    Cherished : 21 writers on animals they have loved and lost / [edited by]
Barbara Abercrombie.
        p.   cm.
ISBN 978-1-57731-957-3 (pbk.)
    1. Pets—Anecdotes. 2. Pet owners—Anecdotes. 3. Human-animal
relationships—Anecdotes. I. Abercrombie, Barbara.
SF416.C44 2011
636.088'7—dc22   2011001426

First printing, April 2011
ISBN 978-1-57731-957-3
Printed in Canada on 100% postconsumer-waste recycled paper

g New World Library is a proud member of the Green Press Initiative.

10 9 8 7 6 5 4 3 2 1

For Gillan

Arthritic and weak, my old dog Hattie
stumbles behind me over the snow.
When I stop, she stops, tipped to one side
like a folding table with one of the legs
not snapped in place. Head bowed, one ear
turned down to the earth as if she
could hear it turning, she is losing the trail
at the end of her fourteenth year.
Now she must follow. Once she could catch
a season running and shake it by the neck
till the leaves fell off, but now they get away,
flashing their tails as they bound off
over the hill. Maybe she doesn't see them
out of those clouded, wet brown eyes,
maybe she no longer cares. I thought
for a while last summer that I might die
before my dogs, but it seems I was wrong.
She wobbles a little way ahead of me now,
barking her sharp small bark,
then stops and trembles, excited, on point
at the spot that leads out of the world.

—— TED KOOSER

CONTENTS

PREFACE

Robert Goldman, DVM

I'm a family veterinarian: a general practitioner for dogs and cats. (And occasionally rabbits, guinea pigs, mice, rats, lizards, turtles, snakes, and birds.) I vaccinate and deworm puppies and kittens, then spay or neuter them before they reach maturity. I open cats' abscesses and close lacerations on dogs who lose a conflict with another animal (or a window). For complicated geriatric conditions such as cancer, cataracts, or cardiac failure, I refer my patients and their humans to veterinary specialists in oncology, ophthalmology, and cardiology. And when my patients have reached the end of their journey and need help to ease their suffering, I put them to sleep.

Watching animals die is by far the worst part about being a veterinarian. Even under the best circumstances lies the knowledge that a wonderful creature's life is ending, and that a good person is suffering an unspeakable loss and entering a world of pain.

I offer Kleenex, a cup of water, a touch on the arm, a kind word. None of it ever seems adequate. I retreat to the back room while the clients suffer in private.

I mail sympathy cards, sometimes send flowers or make a donation in the deceased pet's name. I occasionally offer referrals to grief counselors. For those who lose a pet to circumstances other than death, such as theft or divorce or behavior issues, there is also little or no consolation.

In twenty years of being a veterinarian, I've lost tens of thousands of patients. I've lost patients who became friends, friends who became patients, and I've lost my own beloved pets. This whole time I've been searching for a book such as this one for my own consolation and to share with my clients.

Pet loss is such a difficult and painful topic to think about, let alone discuss. There is still a stigma attached to grieving over an animal. Yet so many clients tell me how they cried harder over the loss of their dogs or cats than they did over the loss of their parents or spouses. Those who grieve for animals often encounter avoidance. Avoidance adds pain. Acknowledgment of their loss is what they need.

In this book, writers acknowledge their own losses. They write about wonder dogs, fractious cats, retired horses, and affectionate pigs. These writers find meaning in the chaos of losing a beloved animal friend. I hope that, like me, you find comfort in this loving and unsentimental homage to the animals in our lives.

INTRODUCTION

Barbara Abercrombie

We ride stories like rafts,
or lay them out on the table like maps.

— WILLIAM KITTRIDGE

The idea for this book came when my twenty-six-year-old horse, Robin, had to be put down because of acute laminitis. I adored this horse. He was a sorrel fox trotter with a white teardrop on his forehead and *U.S.* branded on his flank — a souvenir from working as a trail horse for the U.S. Forest Service. My husband bought him at auction for five hundred dollars, and he came to live out his retirement at our place in Montana. I knew nothing about horses, and frankly I was past the age when anyone sane takes up horseback riding for the first time, but I fell in love with Robin. He was so patient, so forgiving, that he made me feel like his own personal horse whisperer.

I wrote about his death on my blog, saying how much I had loved him and how hard I was grieving for him. I received a lot of comments, including one from a veterinarian friend who suggested there should be an anthology of such pieces about the love and loss of an animal. I realized this was the kind of book I wanted to read — how other animal lovers got through their loss, how they made meaning out of it. Grieving for an animal can be a pretty lonely place.

So I wrote to writers whose work I admired, both friends and strangers, and asked if they'd contribute essays for this book. Everybody responded, passionate about the stories of their animals — the funny, crazy parts, as well as the grief at the end of the animal's life or when they had to give the animal up for reasons beyond their control. They brought so many different angles to my original idea that this anthology grew deeper and far richer than I had originally imagined.

I've always lived with an animal — or multiple animals. When my daughters were growing up, we had three dogs, four cats, and a rabbit. One of the dogs was a Newfoundland named Jennifer who was the size of a small bear and loved to sleep in our bed with her huge head on the down pillows. One of the cats, Crazy Alice, insisted on sleeping in our bathroom sink. Another cat, Yeager, got hit by a car, had his pelvis crushed and rebuilt, along with an expensive tail amputation, and then, after he recovered, raced out into traffic again to have his jaw shattered, and once more survived. (Our cats then became indoor cats.) And Sidney, the youngest of the cat gang, would fish tampon tubes out of wastepaper baskets and then appear jauntily holding one in his mouth as if smoking a cigarette.

Then there was Winesburg — the cat I rescued in New York when I was still a teenager. When she died almost two decades later, we had been on a long journey together, both in miles and time — half my life in fact.

Here's the thing about losing animals: they take a piece of your life with them when they die. They love the best in you, they share your days and nights, and then they're gone and there's a hole in your life — this vanished past they've taken with them.

In California I live with two elderly cats, Stuart and Charlotte, who joined me as kittens when I was newly divorced and then became my bridge through single life to a second marriage. They're now eighteen years old. Stuart, the bon vivant of the feline world, has failing kidneys, and Charlotte, his shy sister, is diabetic, requiring two insulin shots a day. I worry about them. But I think one of the lessons animals can teach you is how to live in the moment; and at this moment, as I type these words, they're happily sprawled on my desk, purring in the sun.

Last summer when I returned to Montana, I visited Robin's grave out in the pasture by the river — this dear valiant horse whose gentleness and patience gave me the gift of knowing and loving a horse, who made me a whole lot braver than I actually was. I remembered how he smelled of wind and hay, the softness behind his ears, the way he'd nuzzle me when he hadn't seen me for a while — and gratitude began to move the sadness out of my heart.

IN THE FOLLOWING PAGES, twenty-one writers put into words what it's like to love an animal — in all its joy, frustration, craziness, humor, grief, and gratitude.

During World War II, Joe Morgenstern's parents found a unique way to get rid of his beloved childhood dog: he remembers how Mr. Fluff was enrolled in Dogs for Defense for the war effort. Billy Mernit, though terrified of pit bulls, fell in love with his new wife's pit bull, Molly, and, he writes, "I was her dutiful bitch in no time." Jane Smiley sat by her horse's body after he was put down, and writes of staying with him "long enough to recognize that he was not there, that this body was like a car he had driven and now had gotten out of."

Judith Lewis Mernit's two dogs, who died within a week of each other at age seventeen, taught her about conflict, love, and loyalty, causing her to revise what she thought she knew of their relationship and what she herself knew about love. Robin Romm found a stray she adored who embodied hope for her, but she had to give the puppy up when her other dog, named Mercy, terrorized it. When one of Thomas McGuane's horses had to be put down, his veterinarian told him that "we had to change our perspective and try to understand that animals accept what happens to them. And it's not as if they don't know. They know." Jenny Rough fell in love with a photograph of an old cat with kidney disease up for adoption on the Internet, and learned something important about herself from her obsession with her virtual cat.

When her dog died at home, Anne Lamott felt that "something huge, a tide, had washed in, and then washed out." Carolyn See remembers the coyote mix who appeared, starving and thin, in the canyon where she lived, and how with time and love, Isha became part of the family, turning into a coyote diva and turning Carolyn's daughter Lisa into a love slave. Michael Chitwood, preparing for his new creative writing class by finding quotes about "why we write and what the real subjects of writing should be," periodically went out to check on his ailing sixteen-year-old cat, The General. "The General's story will be concluded," he writes, "but it won't be finished. That may be the truest thing about a story. Even when it's over, it's not over."

IF YOU'RE AN ANIMAL LOVER, you have stories. I hope our stories deepen and confirm your understanding and love of animals, entertain you and make you laugh, and also comfort you if you've recently lost a pet. C. S. Lewis once wrote, "We read to know we are not alone." On the following pages are the stories of kindred souls who have cherished their animals, mourned their deaths, and eventually learned from them what's truly important in life.

ISHA

Carolyn See

Whe my life partner, John Espey, and I first moved into a new little house in Topanga Canyon, we found ourselves out in the sticks — literally. It was a rough part of the canyon, arid, parched, unwelcoming. John killed maybe six rattlesnakes in the first two weeks. Tarantulas jumped in the basement. Scorpions were plentiful. It was, as my old Texan dad would say, hotter than a policeman's pistol. My daughters, eighteen-year-old Lisa and eight-year-old Clara, were highly skeptical of the whole project. I think we all had second thoughts in those first weeks. This was the first time we'd tried to live together as a family.

Raccoons, possum, more snakes of the harmless kind. Our house was at the top of a cliff, at one end of a crescent of raw earth. From the back our view was literally endless. In front, a narrow road ended in a cul-de-sac. Every night at the end of the crescent, maybe a dozen coyotes gathered to howl. And there was another animal, not readily identifiable — probably half coyote, half German shepherd — starved down to the bone, cowering, skulking, skidding back into the underbrush whenever she saw one of us looking at her. But she began to look marginally better after a few weeks. That was because separately we'd all been feeding her on the sly.

John named her Isha, a feminization of the Indian name Ishi, which was the name of the last member of an Indian tribe that Kroeber, the anthropologist, had immortalized. But Isha had it better than Ishi, by far. Since she played so infernally hard to get (what else could she do, really? She was wild, she was mad as a March hare), we competed slavishly for her attention, talking baby talk to her, handing her little treats, trying mightily to get her to eat from our hands. All this took weeks. And it took over a year to coax her inside the house. People anthropomorphize their pets all the time, and it's a trait I scorn in others, but it was hard not to project human meaning on her diva ways. She was mistress of the injured look. She cringed every time she got near John, until he raised his voice to a falsetto. "She must have been mistreated when she was young," he said, but who was really to know? She'd already had one litter of pups before we knew her; during that first year when she prowled the borders of our house, she had another — she ate a few and squashed the rest. She had a different frame of mind than the rest of us.

Finally she'd come inside the house, but the house was tall and narrow — three stories. The living room was eight steps up from the kitchen: what a production to cajole and wheedle and generally carry on to get her to the living room level! We all adored her, but her plain favorite was Lisa, who was as hard to get as she was; they spent time giving each other scornful looks. But then as we'd be watching television, John and I on one couch, Lisa and Clara on the other, Isha would come up and lay her head on Lisa's knee. Lisa would reciprocate by bopping Isha on her snout (can't there be a prettier word for the space between a dog's eyes and her nose?), bopping her gently but negligently, then doing it with more and more decision, until it might have been called abuse by an animal rescue person, but Isha loved it, pushing her head up under Lisa's hand, wanting more. It had a particular sound, like a champagne cork coming out; celebratory.

Stories about pets often carry something silly and intrinsically embarrassing about them. Lisa, a bestselling novelist now, used to spend fifteen minutes bopping Isha's nose, while we all watched fondly? Unimaginable, really. But once, when I was cleaning up the living room, Isha was sitting on the couch and I wanted to sweep off the dog hair. I said "Down, Isha," and said it again. And again. Then I put my hand to her body to give her a little shove. She laid back her ears and snarled, showing all her teeth, and she wasn't a dog anymore. She was Isha, and she could lie on the couch as much as she wanted. She was also Isha when the coyotes, about ten o'clock at night, would gather in the cul-de-sac or out on the crescent and howl, and Isha, living her dog life, would pause on a landing and pitch back her head and howl along with them. I would watch the hair on my forearms rise up.

One morning a Chinese moving man brought a new easy chair for the living room. The house, as I've said, was on three levels — the kitchen at ground level, then eight steps up to the living room, then another eight to where the bedrooms were. The chair was enormous, and John helped him push and pull the thing from the kitchen level up those first eight stairs. John took the "up" side, pulling the chair with all his might. The moving man took the "down" side, pushing the chair up. His muscles strained; his legs were bowed. Isha was outside, but the door to the house was open. As I watched from the kitchen, she sped past me so quickly I couldn't focus on her, ran up about four stairs and chomped down from behind on the mover's defenseless crotch. Then she hurtled back out again.

The mover, in the living room by this time, let out an ungodly yowl and yanked down his pants, sure he'd been castrated. John and I were mortified, and also afraid he'd sue us for everything we had, which would have been totally appropriate. But the poor guy, once he found himself in one piece, only said mournfully, "It's because I'm Chinese. Some animals don't like that smell." We weren't going to argue with him.

She was wild! We had to learn it over and over again. By this time she would jump on our beds and cover us with "kisses," and push at Lisa to bop her on the head, and greet our cars coming up the driveway with all the doglike signals of delight. One day we gave an afternoon party full of journalists, and one of them, Digby Diehl, brought along his daughter, Dylan, a pretty but willful little girl. I went out into the yard to stock up on more lemons for rum drinks, and Dylan ran out and put her arms around Isha. Isha laid back her ears and stiffened. Dylan was still small, so that her throat was just about at a level with Isha's teeth. I remembered the Chinese mover and was filled with dread. "Dylan,"

I said in the low voice you reserved in Topanga for talking in front of rattlesnakes, "let go of the dog and come over here." Of course, Dylan tightened her grip. Isha began making a noise. "Dylan, the dog is dangerous. Take your hands off her, and come over here!" That little girl wouldn't do shit. It took four or five attempts, and to this day Dylan doesn't know how close she was to an unpleasant death.

The question comes up: Why did we keep her? We were crazy in love with her is the answer. But I don't think it was for all those "unconditional love" reasons you hear when people talk about their beloved pets. I think it was more the part of her that would happily tear the balls off a Chinese mover, or eat up a few of her pups because she was hungry or she felt like it. The part of her that left Dylan Diehl alive only by whim, the reach into a world we don't talk about but know is there — the part that's acknowledged by a howl, and not by any means a heartbroken howl — in the depths of the night.

Remember that when we moved in together, good manners had to be the order of the day, and they were. Maybe Isha made all that good behavior bearable.

About thirteen years after all this started, Isha died. The household had changed. Lisa had married a deeply respectable husband and was living a life of extreme rectitude. She had children and a fine career. Sweet little Clara was old enough to be in college and have a darling boyfriend, Chris. John had changed from a man strong and sure of himself into a tentative person in the last four years of his life. He fainted frequently, walked slowly, seemed far away. I remember myself as brash and pathetically ignorant of the fact that the best times in my life were about to be ending — the years with John, the whole freewheeling existence that was Topanga, all of it.

John and I went to Australia for a couple of weeks. John said later he'd said good-bye to Isha, but I left without a thought. Things were the way they were, just swell. Nothing else crossed my mind. Several days passed before we even got in touch with Clara, who was taking care of the house with Chris. They had woken up one morning to find Isha really ill. Had gone down to the general store to get some ground meat for nourishment. It was one of those monumental August-in-Topanga days — about 120 degrees. Out by the side of the house, in the dirt, Isha died in Clara's arms.

Clara and Chris dug a hole in the brick-hard ground out on the crescent, wrapped Isha in an afghan that had belonged to Lisa's old boyfriend, a Vietnam vet, and covered the grave with large flat stones to keep the coyotes away. Then they called Lisa, who was heartbroken. In a few minutes, Lisa called back. "Are you sure that dog's dead?" she asked. And then, in a few more minutes, the phone rang again: Chris picked up this time, and Lisa impersonated me. "This is Carolyn See. I'm calling about my dog, Isha. Are you sure she's OK?" And finally, one last call to Clara: "FYI, Clara, you know mom and John have only been gone a few days. And then the neighbors see you and your boyfriend digging a shallow grave out on the point. Don't you think they'd be justified in calling the cops?"

Just Lisa, bopping Isha's head in the last way she knew, the sound of a champagne cork opening at a party that's already stopped.

2.

A STORY ABOUT THE GENERAL

Michael Chitwood

I'm preparing for the first meeting of my creative writing class this semester. What I've been doing so far this morning is selecting a group of quotes I want to hand out. The quotes, from famous writers, are about why we write and what the real subjects of writing should be. They offer tips about the best way to get emotion into your fiction and poetry, mostly, it seems, by not looking directly at it.

Every hour or so, I take a break from quote harvesting and go out to the garage. Our sixteen-year-old cat is curled on a blanket out there. He has an awkward cast on one of his hind legs. I broke the cat's leg three days ago when I accidentally backed over him in my car. The cat is deaf, or nearly so. He was sleeping under the car and must not have heard it crank. I felt the little bump of the wheel going over his leg and then saw him limp away, dragging one useless leg.

James Merrill says, "You hardly ever need to *state* your feelings. The point is to feel and keep the eyes open. Then what you feel is expressed, is mimed back at you by the scene."

After the first day in the cast, the cat — his name is General Sterling Price, after a cat in a John Wayne movie — did not move off his blanket. I have to put his food on a little paper plate and place it near his head. He eats what he can reach without getting up and then pulls the plate closer with one paw. Once I came out and he was asleep with his head in the plate.

Charles Wright says, "What you have to say — though ultimately all-important — in most cases will not be news. How you say it just might be."

On the day I broke the cat's leg, my fourteen-year-old son said, "This cat has been with us for all my life." Though he said it in a surprised tone, as if he'd just realized that fact, I thought, thanks, that's something I really needed to hear.

Before the accident, The General — for some reason we always referred to him with the article — was looking elderly. He had lost weight and was finicky about what he ate. Like I said, he had mostly lost his hearing, and his eyesight wasn't great. A little dog in our neighborhood would sometimes escape from his fence and come to bark at The General. The General would be asleep in his favorite spot and the dog would come up behind and let go a tremendous chorus of soprano barking. The General would continue to sleep peacefully.

"All you need is one emotion and four walls for a short story," says Willa Cather.

The General doesn't like it in the garage. He's an outdoor cat. The first day he was in the garage, he would drag himself toward the door when I opened it to get the car out. In his youth, he was a real fighter, a night prowler. I know for a fact that he once tangled with a raccoon and held his own. He would slink in mornings with patches of fur missing or a gash in his shoulder. His ears are ragged as old battle flags.

Even as a kitten, The General was the bold sort. One Saturday afternoon when we had had him for only about two weeks, I was lying in a hammock in our backyard. The General, just a little orange rag of a thing, was chasing down grasshoppers. I think I dozed for a bit. Then I heard The General's plaintive meowing. At first, I couldn't locate him. Then I saw him perched on a limb of the pine that held up one end of the hammock. He was twenty, thirty feet off the ground.

I didn't have a ladder that long. The trunk of the tree was limbless nearly up to where The General was stranded. He was starting to panic, and so was I. I dashed into the house and grabbed a pillow from our bed. I got back just in time to see the kitten hanging by his forepaws on the limb. His claws lost their grip, and I caught him in the pillow, a Hail Mary for sure. He seemed unfazed and went back to stalking grasshoppers.

Just now I had to clean up a place in the garage where he crawled off the blanket and urinated.

"It begins with a character usually," William Faulkner says. "Once he stands up on his feet and begins to move, all I do is trot along behind him with a paper and pencil [or pillow] trying to keep up long enough to put down what he says and does."

When my son was an infant, The General, when we weren't looking, got into his crib and peed on his head. I think the cat was feeling ignored, and probably territorial with this new animal. Though neutered, The General always remained a tom, aggressive, combative. When we played the catch-the-string game, I would suddenly find him halfway up my arm, his claws fastened to the sleeve of my shirt. He played rough and would quickly lay flat his ears and yowl threateningly. He was a biter. Given all that, and his dislike of our newborn, The General became a full-time outdoor cat.

"A story always involves, in a dramatic way, the mystery of personality," according to Flannery O'Connor.

We moved from our small starter home when The General was about four years old. He had been curious about all the boxes and commotion of moving, but curious only in the offhand way of cats, sniffing a crate of books or climbing through the maze of a disassembled bed. I had devised a plan for how we would move him. He would be the last thing to go. When we had everything ready at the new place, I put him in a cardboard box. Except for his first ride to our house as a tiny kitten, he'd never been in a car before, because we had a vet who would actually make house calls (it was his marketing pitch). So, I got The General in the box and we went to the new house, some eight to ten miles away.

"A poem is one of the few opportunities you have to say two things at once," according to Robert Frost. "For me the initial delight is in the surprise of remembering something I didn't know I knew. No surprises for the poet, no surprises for the reader."

After three days, The General disappeared. Not even the old trick we had of shaking the treat box would bring him running. We shook the treat box all over our new neighborhood. We put up signs and offered a reward. We called "Gennnnneral" as we walked, like frightened soldiers calling for their leader. But to no avail.

The next week the people we had sold our old house to called. "Didn't you have a big orange cat?" the man wanted to know. "Yes," I said.

"Well, he's here. He's hanging around in the shrubs." The General had not been able to see the route we took to the new house. He would have had to cross a sizable creek, railroad tracks, and a half-dozen busy roads to get home. How he did it I will never know. I retrieved him, and he decided that the new place was home.

The General has pretty much stopped drinking. He'll lap up a little milk if I put the bowl under his chin. The broken leg has developed an infection. When I took him in for the cast, the vet said that his kidneys were failing. He hasn't moved off the blanket for two days, other than to try to pull clear of it to relieve himself. I know how this story is going to end. Pretty soon, I've got to decide when it will end. The General's story will be concluded, but it won't be finished. That may be the truest thing about a story. Even when it's over, it's not over.

3.

HOPE

Robin Romm

Last night I dreamed I placed a classified ad. "New home needed for our cattle dog, Mercy." A kid came over sporting a backward baseball cap and baggy shorts, his body language spastic. "Totally!" he belted. "Totally! I love dogs! I'll take her!" And before I could hand her over — the canine love of my life, her smell like bark-o-mulch and oil, her rounded forehead and puppy eyes — I woke up with a start.

"That is a horrible dream," said my boyfriend, Don. He looked at me ruefully, judgmentally, as if I'd actually done it, given away the one being that reliably gave us joy.

The dream could have been fueled by the conference I'd returned from the night before. My friend Jim lost his dog while he was there. His daughter had called him at six AM, crying. "My dog died," he kept saying. And people stopped briefly to tilt their heads and make sorry eyes. But nobody grabbed him in a feverish embrace or wept. I imagined losing our Mercy, and a cold pang went through me. "I'm so sorry," I said. "I don't know how we'd manage if we lost our dog." I must have looked horrified, because Jim smiled at me.

"You guys are really attached to Mercy, aren't you?" he said as we rode the escalator down through a light-filled convention center.

"We don't have kids," I said.

"Yeah, before we had kids I guess we were really attached to our dogs, too."

Or maybe the dream hurled itself from deeper in my subconscious. Before I was born, my parents had a vizsla, Major. Our refrigerator still honors a picture of him, his strong, athletic build; muscles that rippled when he ran; brick red coat; and golden eyes. My mother returned from her teaching job each afternoon to throw a ball into a field for him, over and over and over — the dog that, like Mercy, was supposed to get her past the heartache of moving from Brooklyn to Nashville, to Salt Lake City, to Eugene. The dog galloped and returned, galloped and returned, until his eyes grew grateful, his body leaden, and he and my mother would retire to the brown velvet sofa.

Then I was born, and the dog's life changed. One day, when I was two, I ran into my bedroom squawking, holding a box of Cheerios in my hand. Major, asleep under my crib, startled awake and, in a flash, ripped the skin under my eye. I have no memory of this, but all my baby pictures prove it — that ugly plum-colored scar underlining my eye socket.

"It wasn't a difficult decision," my mom said. They took Major to the vet that day and put him to sleep.

But I've always wondered about it, the actual scene. Something about my mother's lack of emotion struck me, even as a kid, as inauthentic. How could it not have been difficult, traumatic, to lose the dog that had been their baby for so many years? And I wondered, though I never asked, if she stayed with Major when they injected the fluid. Did he look at her with those trusting golden eyes as he grew strangely sleepy?

Or the dream is an amalgam, taken partly from these cues, and partly from another story about a childhood dog. A story I don't really want to revisit, even for the time it will take to write an essay. It's a story that requires a bit of history.

My mother died after a nine-year illness — and after she died, I threw myself, deeply shocked and exhausted, into work. I wrote in the mornings, and in the afternoons, six days a week, I taught. Composition, vocabulary building, literature, fiction writing, and memoir writing. In a short time, I parlayed this frenzy of activity into a book deal and a tenure-track teaching job in Santa Fe, New Mexico.

In retrospect, it's easy to see that I was looking for solid ground, a new center to my life now that my mother, once the sun I orbited, was gone. It would be this job in Santa Fe. So Don and I sold most of our stuff for pennies, loaded a moving truck, put Mercy in the car, and went in search of a life.

It was nothing like I'd imagined. It was an unmitigated disaster.

We'd rented a house quickly, in a weekend. It was cute. A converted barn in the hills north of town. The landlady was a slow-moving, New Age therapist, and the house, we learned later, had been built on a lark by a man who'd left her years ago. We were novices to Santa Fe, and didn't realize the barn was built directly on the dust in a depression beneath a steep slope. In other words, the house was in a drainage ditch below the landlady's much nicer house — that solid structure with a view. Before renting it, we didn't look for gaps that would let in critters, rain, snow, freezing air, hot air, dust. We didn't ask about the cost of propane heat in a house full of holes — and whether cathedral ceilings were a good idea in a house heated that way.

The first week there, the monsoon came. The rains pelted this poorly built barn, and in came water, brown with dust. It came under our doors, through our vents and the old stovepipe over the bed. Rivers ran over the slate tiles. Then came the bugs, seeking shelter from the rain. A spider the size of a baseball, a pinkish scorpion, a centipede the size of a serving spoon. Our well broke, turning our water into blood-colored silt, which, because of the dirt in it, caused our toilet, sink, washer, and dishwasher to break, one by one. When the washing machine failed in the middle of the night, it filled our house with inches of water. (I woke with Mercy nestled next to me, gazing down as if from a raft.) Our heaters, it turned out, were spitting out carbon monoxide. (We survived, ironically, because of the holes in our walls.) And then, when we — too tired to move again — asked for a rent reduction, our landlady declared that we "were not a match" and terminated our lease.

Meanwhile, the job that brought us there fell apart. First, the college said it was broke. They would be laying people off. Then they declared exigency. Eventually, a year and a half later, they closed.

I offer you this so you can imagine my hopefulness, my vulnerability, my frailness. So you can see what I might have seen the day she appeared, this small white and black puppy. She stood nosing a pile of garbage in front of a dilapidated adobe down the street from the new house we rented downtown. We were walking Mercy when I spotted her. She paused and looked at me. Her eyes were a glossy black. Her nose was oddly indented, flat like a pig's and mottled with pink. She had the body of a dachshund and the head of some sort of terrier. Her legs were bowed, feet turned out like a duck's, and she had an underbite so large you could have put a bar of soap on it.

Some neighborhood kids were in their yard.

"Is this your dog?" I asked. They shook their heads.

"A stray, I think," the little boy said, wielding a toy gun. "Been around here for a few days." The pup had no collar, and you could see her ribs.

I paused, afraid to walk over to her — afraid that she would dart away or bite. The little girl flipped her long hair over one shoulder and put a hand on her hip. "You want it?" she asked. I didn't know what to say, but before I could begin overthinking the situation, she knelt. "Come on," she said to the puppy, patting her knees. The puppy jumped to its hind legs. She scooped it up and thrust it at me.

People describe love this way — that chemical *yes*. The way the brain turns off and the heart turns on, and all you want is the smell of the beloved. This little ferret dog with her weird feet and wiry fur rested smoothly against my chest. She looked at me, those doggie questions in her eyes. And out came a tiny pink tongue, like a petal. She kissed me right there, no reservations.

"What are you doing?" Don asked again. He stood across the street with Mercy, who had begun to growl.

"We can't just leave her here," I said. How could I convince him? I could tell from the locked-up look on his face that he was not experiencing the same thing as me. He was not in the throes of a magic spell.

"She's cute, Robin, but she's probably somebody's dog." The pup put a paw on my shoulder so she could get a better look at him. She cocked her head. Don took out his phone and called the animal shelter.

"Can't she stay the night?" I asked.

"Robin, you found her on the street. We should take her in so someone can claim her. Also, she's in heat," he said. She looked too young to be in heat, but when I took a closer look it was true. I held her so that part wasn't as visible.

In the end, I swaddled the dog in towels and we got in the car. The ride to the shelter was long. The pup stretched out in my lap, paws dangling over my knees, and fell asleep. The road turned bumpy and she woke, climbed down to my feet, and licked each toe. She looked up sleepily a few times, full of thanks and trust.

When we got to the counter, I couldn't hand her over. A woman was getting rid of a large black Rottie mix that bit her boyfriend. The pup peered over my arms, alert and curious.

"Robin, you're being unreasonable," Don said. "It's a little dog, and someone might come and claim her. If not, she'll get adopted fast. You know I love dogs, but let's prepare for a puppy if we're going to get one."

But it was clear, even to Don, who was overwhelmed by deadlines and his father's grave illness: I needed solid ground. And if it wasn't to be Santa Fe or a job at a college, if it wasn't to be my mother or anything else, well it was going to be that little dog with the smashed face and underbite. I would rescue her and she would rescue us — the way Mercy had when my mother died — and then we would be whole.

I buried my nose in the puppy's fur all the way home, hiding tears. We'd done our duty, filled out a found report, but we still had her, the unexpected answer to our problems. Don looked resigned. He reached over to scratch her terrier scruff.

Rain began to pour, that big desert sky cracking open, the giant drops obscuring our view. I concocted a plan. I would walk Mercy for an hour, try to wear her out, and then Don and I would do an introduction. What could go wrong? The puppy had a lovely temperament. Mercy had a wise soul — this was my closest animal friend, the same dog who the day of my mother's funeral watched the house fill with people in high heels offering false comfort, and, though she'd never chewed anything before, chewed a hole through the bedroom wall. *Let's get out of here*, she seemed to say, and nothing could have felt more in tune. She is my mutt, the master of metaphor, the largest love, the star of the hiking trail. These dogs would understand that together they could be twice as powerful, twice as distracting, twice as capable of large and heroic acts.

When I returned from the walk with Mercy, the puppy was waiting for us at the gate. I didn't see her little white body, and before I could stop her, Mercy roared and lunged, pinning the puppy against the wall, growling and snapping. The pup squealed, over and over, like a piglet being slaughtered, her body flat against the adobe. Don ran out. "No no no!" we cried. Shaken, Don pulled Mercy away. The hair around her neck bristled, and her eyes, usually so accepting, were flat as a bear's. The little dog hid between my legs, her black eyes filled with soft terror.

For hours we sat with the dogs under the covered patio, watching the rain, watching the dogs watch each other. We quieted them. But if we loosened Mercy's leash, she lunged. Don looked worried.

"This is not going to work," he said. "I told you."

We didn't yet own a crate, so I spent the night in my office, on our pullout sofa with the puppy. She followed me around the room, a little piece of my shadow, wagging her body furiously every time I talked to her. "Do you want to live here?" I'd ask. WAG. "Do you like this sofa?" WAG. "Is this true love?" WAG WAG WAG. And when I stretched out to sleep, she hopped on the bed, stretched out beside me, and conked out. I felt her heat against my chest and thought of names. Hope, Sprout, Devonne. Mercy had been difficult at first, too, lunging at our cats. Growling. This would pass, and she, this Hope, would be mine.

In the morning, the puppy ran in circles, her tongue stuck in her underbite, pink and wet. I taught her to walk on a leash, a skill she lacked, by luring her with cheese. She seemed proud of her accomplishment. Though she was a good-natured dog, it was me she preferred. Unlike Mercy, who would collapse for a belly rub in front of absolutely anyone, this dog reserved her distilled delight for me.

And so I fell completely under her spell. I held her tiny body against my chest and felt her heartbeat, soft under her fur. She showed up in my life at the precise moment it was falling apart. It mattered. She mattered. I couldn't lose her.

But the problems with Mercy persisted. No matter how happy or calm I made the situation, if the puppy was near, Mercy immediately gave her the whale eye and lunged, sounds of murderous rage coming from deep inside her.

Our friend from the animal shelter came over to help. "You'd have a long, dangerous road," she said after two hours of awkward play at a fenced baseball field that ended in snarls. "Your dog just doesn't like this puppy." I called a trainer. "You have a territorial heeler with a prey drive. My guess is, you should find that little dog a loving home before the bloodbath ensues."

I couldn't sleep. How could this be true? No one had come looking for this puppy. I'd posted ads and filled out the reports. It had clearly been fate that she stopped to smell trash right near our house after an epically bad year. The nights I slept with Don and Mercy in the bedroom, I got up repeatedly to visit the puppy in the new crate in my office, and every time, our reunion was ecstatic, full of heat and wild joy.

But Don kept insisting that this dog could have a great life with another family — a family that didn't have a dog who wanted to kill her. In addition, his eyes were itching. He felt allergic to her fur. All the dog people were telling me that two females have a hard time living together, that bring-ing a bitch in heat into the house with another female was unwise. During summer, I had the time to walk them sepa-rately, pet them separately — live a two-dog life. But once my teaching job started up in the fall, I'd be screwed.

After a particularly bad day of trying to get the dogs to sit in the living room together (which ended with me bawl-ing on the sofa, unable to understand why Mercy would want to prevent the exponential increase in animal love in our home), I emailed the staff at the college. My love for this dog must have come out in the writing, because in only an hour, I had twelve replies. A man came by, crazy for dogs, and was delighted by her underbite and the cute way she rolled and showed her belly. He claimed he'd take her home for an hour, introduce her to his dog, wife, and child. I reluc-tantly gave her to him, assuming I'd have her back later that day and could try with Mercy a few more times.

Three hours later, the man phoned. The dog fit perfectly into their family. She followed their kid around, delighted. She rubbed up against their gentle coonhound. They needed to know if I was going to take this dog back. Already, he said, his wife was attached. The dog was lying at his wife's hip. Everything was happy, peaceful, safe.

What was it I wanted?

I stammered. I stumbled. I said I would call them back.

For a while, I sat dumbly on the sofa, staring at the font on the phone book. I wanted the dog to save me, but wasn't it the dog who needed saving?

The week following my decision, I waited with bated breath every time the phone rang, hoping it would be the family saying they'd changed their minds. That puppy and I were destined to make this work. I had to believe it. But they didn't call. I emailed the man asking about her. He emailed back saying that all was well. Did I want to visit her? They'd named her Frida, after Frida Kahlo, saying they both were "almost attractive."

No. No, I didn't want to visit. I'd like to say that I rose above it, that I took the high road. Frida was out of harm's way, our rapture on the fold-out sofa bed lost in her doggie mind. She, like all dogs, existed solely in the present. But it wasn't that easy for me.

Because that puppy wasn't simply a puppy. She was all the things I yearned for but couldn't have: a mother, a death-free young adulthood, a safe home, a solid job. She was Hope, and she, too, had been wrested from me the moment she came into view.

A few days later, Don and I went to a party on a mesa overlooking a crystalline river. It was a New Mexico early fall, the sun pouring so feverishly over rock and shrub that it did away with shadow.

"What did you end up doing with that *creature*?" my friend asked in his South African accent. He'd been teasing me about my strange bond with what he claimed was the world's ugliest animal. And there on that wooden bench in a crowd of festively dressed people on that perfect day, I cried.

I cried chopping carrots, sitting on the sofa, reading, in bed. Don hugged me, gave me tissues. He promised me other dogs. He promised me his undying affection. But nothing soothed me.

And Mercy. For a while I couldn't touch her, couldn't be near her. "Go away," I commanded this dog I had rescued from the Merced pound, who had stayed loyally by my side through my mother's death and all the tumult that followed. She'd betrayed me, acted in her own interest.

I sulked. No one quite believed the depths of my grief. That dog? My friends laughed. The piggy one with the messed up jaw?

She wasn't dead. She wasn't sick. She was happily trotting behind that coonhound in the nice house of another family.

I remember going to a grief group in Berkeley once, and a woman talked about how she cried when she lost her dog — tears she hadn't cried when her own mother died. The counselor explained that when a parent dies, the loss is often too large for the mind to comprehend. But when a pet dies, we understand it. We see the finality. We experience the loss in smaller, more accessible ways. We can get in touch with that grief — and it touches the shore of that larger island of loss inside us.

So, I gave myself over to it. The loss of the puppy and everything else. I stayed in bed. I wore soft clothes. I failed to return phone calls. I stared at photos I'd taken of her. I prayed the family would call and return her to me. I kept vigilant watch over the neighborhood to see if a sibling of Hope would appear. Then finally, one day, Mercy came over to me and stood stubbornly by my leg.

"Look," she seemed to say. "Look at me." I did. Her round forehead and perked ears. Her tilted head. "Please," said those eyes. "Let's go outside." I sat for a while, then put my hand on her head. She sat, closed her eyes, feeling it there.

It wasn't a softening I felt. It wasn't exactly forgiveness. It was something else — a rising above myself. A sort of metaphysical sigh. I took her red leash out and off we went, into the desert sun.

I got an email just the other day saying that Frida is well. She moved to Washington State after the college in New Mexico closed. I imagine her out there, delirious beneath green trees, as we continue to weather the dust of a new desert city. I imagine her curled at the feet of the child in the family, the way the child gently tugs her ears, the way that translates to Frida as love. It is not the same as death, losing Frida. It bears no relation to the way I will feel the day I lose Mercy (whom I have forgiven, now, completely). It has nothing in common with losing a mother, a grandmother, a grandfather, a friend — all losses I have suffered and somehow survived. But I still have days when I long for her tiny white body in my arms, her strange, smashy face that made everything seem less serious. There are still days when I miss her, or at least the idea of her. The idea that, in the darkest moment, you can find Hope there, pawing through the street garbage. That you can pick her up and hold her. That she can, with a wag of a tail, do away with heartache and show you the way.

4.

MR. T.'S HEART

Jane Smiley

always suspected Mr. T. had one of those large economy-size thoroughbred hearts: maybe not Secretariat size (twenty-two pounds) or Mill Reef size (seventeen pounds), but larger and stronger than average (seven pounds). The horse was a fitness machine.

In five years of riding and eventing, I had never tired him out. He was always ready for more, even if I was nearly falling off him from the exertion.

Every year at his well-horse checkup, the vet would comment on his dropped beats — he could drop two or even three (five seconds between two heartbeats seems like a very long time when the horse is standing before you, apparently alive and well) — and attribute it to the residual effect of a great deal of exercise early in life. (He was a racehorse for eight years and had fifty-two starts.) Thus it was that I wasn't too worried when this year, Mr. T.'s twenty-first, the vet detected what he called arrhythmia. As I was taking another horse up to the vet clinic at UC Davis anyway, I packed Mr. T. along.

The results weren't good. On the one hand, the senior cardiologist shook my hand and thanked me for bringing him a big, lean thoroughbred with a heart that was so efficient and powerful that through the stethoscope it was nearly deafening. On the other hand, that arrhythmia had a name. It was "atrial fibrillation"; and it wasn't just a quirk, it was a potentially dangerous condition. The horse could drop dead at any moment.

I was impressed in spite of myself (and in spite of my conviction that Mr. T. was going to live forever) and agreed to have him "converted" — that is, to allow the cardiologist to administer a powerful and toxic drug, quinidine, that might or might not convert his chaotic heart rhythm to a normal, or "sinus" rhythm. It was an in-patient procedure. I left him there and brought my other horse home.

Mr. T. was a very bad patient. He wouldn't eat, wouldn't relax, would hardly drink. His separation anxiety was so great that the cardiologist actually feared for his survival. He did, however, "convert" — his heart rhythm returned to normal, without any dropped beats — and stayed converted.

The bad news was that the dose it had taken to convert him was very close to toxic. There would be no trying this again. And the quinidine took maybe twice as long to clear his system as usual, putting him at risk in other ways.

I tried not to pay attention to the cardiologist's other remark — that the longer the heart had been arrhythmic, the less likely a permanent conversion. Those dropped beats we had always heard — I wasn't going to admit the possibility that his heart had been arrhythmic as long as I had known him.

Mr. T. had stopped being a jumper — age, an eye injury, and timidity on my part. But not long after I wrote an article about him, "Why I Can't Find a New Horse" in *Practical Horseman*, he started jumping again, and he was great at it, as he had once been — energetic, fast, and full of thrust. And there was no changing his go-for-it style. I'd tried that, and it had just made him confused and anxious. You couldn't parse a fence or a combination or a course and try to get him to jump in a relaxed, easy style. You had to sit up, hold on, and let him do it. It was hugely exciting.

Anyway, two weeks after the conversion, Mike, my local vet, took another EKG. Tick Tock Tick Tock (that was the horse's real name), everything was perfect. I began conditioning Mr. T. for an event at the end of June.

I was well organized in my training, for once. I had him entered in a schooling show, in a couple of jumper classes, and I was galloping him at a local training track once a week. At the beginning of June, I took him over to the track, a half-mile oval. As soon as we entered the gate, he picked up a huge, even, ground-covering trot on very light contact. He trotted happily, his ears pricked, for two miles. Then I walked him half a mile and asked for the canter. For a mile, it was collected, even, easy, a perfect joy. Then I walked him again.

At the last, I gave in to impulse. After he had caught his breath, I turned him, bridged my reins, and assumed galloping position. I said out loud, "Pick your own pace," and he did. He took hold and shot forward, switching leads and going faster about every eighth of a mile, exactly like a racehorse. But then, he was always a racehorse. The other stuff was just for fun.

For me, the "breeze" was both frightening and exhilarating — as fast as I had ever gone on a horse, but incredibly stable. Yes, I was not in control, but he was, and I never doubted that he knew exactly where each foot was at every stride. More important, all this exercise was effortless. He was hardly blowing after we had gone half a mile and I managed to bring him down. It took him the usual ten minutes to cool out.

Three days later, we went to the show. He warmed up and jumped around perfectly, won a couple of ribbons, seemed happy.

Thus it was that I couldn't believe it, four days after that, when Mike told me that his atrial fibrillation was back, and possibly worse. His heart rhythm was chaotic. We took another EKG, sent it off to Davis, discussed it more than necessary with lots of vets. The cardiologist's recommendation was discouraging — walking around, maybe a little trotting from time to time. But, I said. But. But when I galloped him on the track, the work was effortless for him.

The answer to the riddle was in his large, strong heart. He had enough overcapacity to give himself some leeway, to oxygenate himself thoroughly almost all of the time. The danger, to me as well as to him, was that his overcapacity was unpredictable. He could literally be doing fine one moment and drop dead the next. And, the cardiologist suggested, in accordance with the no free-lunch principle, greater-than-average heart size often went with arrhythmia. His recommendation stayed the same — walking, a little jogging from time to time.

I stopped riding the horse. I'm not sure why, except that I was confused and ambivalent. One day I decided to ignore the cardiologist's advice, the next day I decided to heed it. Mr. T. and I were used to working, and working pretty hard. If we weren't allowed to work hard together, then what? I didn't know. I let him hang out in the pasture with his brood-mare friend.

Not too long ago, I decided to pretty much ignore the cardiologist. I wouldn't be stupid and run Mr. T. cross-country or "breeze" him again, but I would do dressage and jump and treat him like a normal horse.

That very day, I went out to give him a carrot, and he was standing in the shade, pawing the ground. I put him in a stall with lots of water and no food — he'd been colicky before. By bedtime, he had manured three or four times.

In the morning he seemed right as rain, so I began introducing a bit of hay. He continued to seem fine. After noon, I let him out. An hour later he was pawing and looking at his flanks. I called Mike, who was engaged but promised to come ASAP.

Half an hour later, the horse was eating manure. My heart sank. Even though Mike and another vet I asked said this meant nothing with regard to colic, I knew differently. I had never seen him do such a thing, and I thought it was an act of equine desperation.

The rest of the day was a losing battle. No matter how much painkiller of whatever kind we gave him, the pain could not be alleviated. And his atrial fibrillation meant that he could not tolerate surgery. The impaction, which may or may not have been a torsion, was out of reach and would not dissolve. At 10:00 PM, I said to Mike, "Are you telling me now's the time?"

He said, "Yes."

I led Mr. T. out of the lighted stall where we had been trying to treat him. He moved, but his head was down and he was hardly conscious of me. We went out into the grassy pasture where he had wandered at large every day of the spring. I knelt down in front of my horse's lowered head, and I told him what a wonderful horse he was, perfect from top to toe every minute. Then Mike gave him the two big shots of barbiturates that would cause him to arrest.

Arrest what?

His heart.

It didn't take more than a second or two. Mike held the lead rope. The collapse of a horse is always earth-shaking. His haunches drop backward, his head flies up, his knees buckle, he falls to the side. We flocked around him, petting and talking to him, but he was gone already.

After everyone left, my boyfriend and I covered him with blankets and went in the house.

I slept fitfully, unable to grasp the suddenness and enormity of the death of my dear friend and constant companion. Each time I woke up, I dreaded going out there at daybreak — what would he look like? How would the mare be acting? What would I do next with a thirteen-hundred-pound body?

When it was finally time to get up, my boyfriend got up with me, and we went out. The mare was in her stall, quiet.

I fed her. Then we approached the mound. Fermentation from the impacted food had already begun — under the blanket, my horse's belly was beginning visibly to swell.

I folded back the cover, expecting something horrible, but Mr. T.'s eyes were closed — a kindness my boyfriend had done me the night before. I can't express how important this was. It was not that I had ever seen his eyes closed before. I had not — he was too alert to sleep in my presence. Rather, it was that, looking familiarly asleep, he looked uniquely at peace.

We sat down next to his head and stroked and petted him and talked. I admired, once again, his well-shaped ears, his beautiful head and throatlatch, his open nostrils, his silky coat, his textbook front legs that raced fifty-two times, in addition to every other sort of equine athletic activity, and were as clean at twenty years old as the day he was born. I admired his big, round, hard feet.

But we didn't just talk to him and about him. We relaxed next to him, stroking and petting, and talking about other things, too. We felt the coolness of his flesh, and it was pleasant, not gruesome. We stayed with him long enough to recognize that he was not there, that this body was like a car he had driven and now had gotten out of. The mare watched us, but she, too, was calm.

Later, when I spoke to the manager of my other mares and foals, she told me that when a foal dies, you always leave it with the mare for a while — long enough for her to realize fully that it is not going to get up again, and to come to terms with that. I thought then that this is true of people, too. We have to experience the absence of life in order to accept it.

My friends know that I adored Mr. T. to a boring and sometimes embarrassing degree. I would *kvell* at the drop of a riding helmet about his every quirk and personal quality. He was a good, sturdy, handsome horse, and a stakes winner, but not a horse of unusual accomplishment or exceptional beauty. He was never unkind and never unwilling — those were his special qualities. Nevertheless, I watched him and doted over him and appreciated him day after day for almost six years.

The result is a surprising one. I miss him less, rather than more. Having loved him in detail (for example, the feel of his right hind leg stepping under me, then his left hind, then his right hind again...for example, the sight of his ears pricking as he caught sight of me over his stall door...for example, the sight of him strolling across his paddock...for example, the feel in my hands of him taking hold and coming under as we approached a fence...for example, the sound of his nicker), I have thousands of clear images of him right with me. I think I miss him less than I thought I would because I don't feel him to be absent.

There is no way to tell non-horsey people that the companionship of a horse is not like that of a dog, or a cat, or a person. Perhaps the closest two consciousnesses can ever come is the wordless simultaneity of horse and rider focusing together on a jump or a finish line or a canter pirouette, and then executing what they have intended together. What two bodies are in such continuous, prolonged closeness as those of a horse and rider completing a hundred-mile endurance ride or a three-day event? I have a friend who characterizes riding as "one nervous system taking over another." I often wonder — which is doing the taking over, and which is being taken over?

I never expected to be writing this essay. Rather, I intended, in twenty years, to write, "Oldest Known Equine Is Seventeen-Hand Ex-Racehorse." But I see it is time to take my own advice, the advice I gave my daughter when she got her first real boyfriend. I told her that no matter what happened with this boyfriend, once she had experienced the joys of a happy and close relationship, she would always know how to have that again, and would always have that again. And the truth is, that works for horses, too.

5.

FLUFF

Joe Morgenstern

Yes, yes, I admit it, I didn't take care of him the way I promised I would.

When I was ten years old, I had a black cocker spaniel named Fluff. (His full name was Mr. Fluff, though he wasn't particularly fluffy: I don't know whether the Mr. was my mother's or my father's idea.) Exactly what I didn't do is lost in the mists of time, but I'm prepared to admit that I didn't walk him enough, didn't clean up after him, didn't feed him regularly, didn't wipe his bowl, didn't check to see that he had water, didn't do any of the things that ten-year-olds promise they will do if their parents will only let them have a dog. The one thing I did do was love him. I can see evidence of that love in the last remaining snapshot I have of him. There I am, standing in front of our suburban New Jersey house in a suit jacket, shirt and tie, and knickers — what was my mother thinking? — and gazing lovingly into

Fluff's eyes as he sits on his hind legs (which he could do, as the stupid pet joke has it, for hours on end). But I don't need the photo to remember how it was between us. I may not have always been there for him, but Fluffy was always there for me, adoring me and, I choose to think, forgiving me for my endless lapses.

My dog is the main subject of this story, but it's also about my mother and father, who found a way to free themselves of having to walk Fluff, feed him, wipe his bowl, etc., etc. They appealed to my patriotism.

The year was 1943, during the darkest days of World War II, when American boys were going off to fight in far-off lands and islands — not just nameless boys, but older brothers of kids I knew. One day my father came home from work in Manhattan, sat down in his big leather chair to read the afternoon paper, and tore an article out from an inside page. The subject, I learned at dinner, was a program just announced by Dogs for Defense.

A civilian organization that provided dogs for military duty, Dogs for Defense had been training large breeds — German shepherds, Doberman pinschers, and the like — as sentry or attack dogs. Now, however, they were planning to train a limited number of small breeds for a very different purpose: going behind enemy lines to find wounded American troops, then leading rescue parties to them. "Wouldn't it be wonderful," my father said, "if they were willing to take Fluff?"

As soon as he said that, I felt a panicky swirl of shock, anxiety, incipient grief, and, God help me, patriotism. I don't know what I said — probably nothing — but over the course of the next few weeks I came around, or was brought around, to the very real possibility that Mr. Fluff might go to war.

If this were a story in an anthology about manipulative parents, I might be reaching right now for my well-worn volumes of Freud, Jung, or Alice Miller. What did my mother and father think they were doing? They were forty years old when I was born, a time when forty meant you were starting to get old. By the time they happened on Dogs for Defense, they may have felt old, and been so preoccupied with the inconvenience of Mr. Fluff that they dared not dwell on the greater inconvenience of my feelings. (I'm giving them a pass here, but this is not an anthology about manipulative parents.) They probably thought they'd discovered a brilliant solution to a nagging problem, and in a sense that was true.

They had me where they wanted me, torn between my love for Fluffy and — I can't believe I'm about to type this, but it's true — my love of country. This was wartime, after all. Kids my age followed the European and Pacific campaigns avidly on the radio, in the newspapers, and in the main source of our emotional information, the war movies. Sending my dog to war had a special cachet, so I buried whatever grief I was feeling when my father told me that arrangements had been made. The army was sending someone to test Mr. Fluff for gun shyness.

A few days later, on a Saturday morning in autumn, an army lieutenant came to our house with a clipboard in his hand and a pistol in his holster. It was only a starter's pistol, but the bespectacled young officer was all business. He took

Mr. Fluff out on the front lawn and told him to sit. Fluff sat. The lieutenant fired a blank round into the air. Fluff continued to sit, awaiting developments. The lieutenant fired again. The second round startled me, but Fluff remained impassive. My dog, the officer declared, had passed his gun-shyness test with flying colors.

A week or so later a sergeant came to take Fluff away in an olive-drab army sedan devoid of chrome. If I said that the moment of my dog's departure was anguishing, I might be telling the truth, but that's not how I remember it. To tell the truly terrible truth, I don't remember the moment very well, but now I'll give myself a pass and say that the boy I was could not have endured such a moment without putting the tightest of lids on his feelings. (At the time, my mother was doing her part for the war effort by cooking with a pressure cooker, which used less gas; the image of that appliance suddenly feels apt for me.) I do remember getting down on the carpet on my hands and knees, holding my dog's sweet warm face close to mine, and giving him a last scratch behind his floppy ears. Then he was gone, and I had nothing to show for him but his leash and collar and his empty bowls.

Nothing, that is, until the following January, when our mailman, Sam, brought a letter, addressed to me and marked WAR DEPARTMENT OFFICIAL BUSINESS. The return address was — or rather, is, since the envelope and its yellowed contents are sitting on my desk as I write this — Assistant K-9 Director, Cat Island RTC, Gulfport, Mississippi. The mimeographed letter, dated 19 January 1944, carries the letterhead HEADQUARTERS, CAT ISLAND WAR DOG RECEPTION AND

TRAINING CENTER. Beneath it is a form message, with a few specifics typed in boldface:

Dear **Sir:**

We are pleased to inform you that your dog named **Fluff,** breed **Cocker Spaniel,** Dogs for Defense No. **New Jersey 501,** has arrived at this center in good condition and has joined other dog recruits in basic training.

You will be further cooperating in the war effort if you will refrain from writing to this Center or to the Quartermaster General requesting information as to the welfare of your dog and the program of its training. While the interest of each individual in his or her dog is a natural one, it is felt that you will readily appreciate the magnitude of the task of furnishing information to the many thousands of donors. You may be assured that your dog is receiving the best of care and attention.

Thanking you for your generosity and interest in furthering the war effort, I am,

Very truly yours,
GEORGE S. PAYSON
1st Lt. Q.M.C.,
Asst. Dir. Of Tng.

I lived on that letter for weeks, all the while furthering the war effort by not writing to Cat Island. (Had there been a Cats for Defense, would the army have done the training on Dog Island?) I did appreciate the magnitude of the task, so I focused my imaginings not on how Fluff was doing as a raw recruit but on how bravely he would behave once he got close to enemy lines and picked up the scent of a fallen soldier.

Early that spring, Sam the mailman brought a delivery slip from Railway Express, the precursor of such freight and package services as FedEx and UPS. The Contents box was blank, but the Sender box said, ominously, "Cat Island War Dog RTC." Because my mother hadn't driven a car since she dented the fender of a Jordan sedan in 1929, I had to wait for my father to come home from work and take me down to the train station. When I presented the slip to the stationmaster, he rummaged around in a storeroom for a while, then emerged with a wooden crate. Inside sat Mr. Fluff, obviously intact and panting with excitement. He went berserk when he saw me, and the feeling was mutual. I was too excited to wonder why he'd come back home so soon, but an explanation eventually arrived in the form of another form letter, still vivid in my memory but no longer in my files. Fluff had failed basic training. No dishonorable behavior was implied, but no details were provided either. In any case, he was a civilian once again, and all mine, once again, to not take care of.

At least for a while. One day my father came home with a big bag of cocktail franks for an impending dinner party. He'd bought them at Ershowsky's — how fateful names stick in the mind! — a Kosher delicatessen on the Lower East Side. (Have I spelled it right? Yes. Through the secular miracle of Google I see that S. Ershowsky and Brothers were on East Houston Street.) My parents were Jewish, but not observant; Kosher delis were the closest they came to temple. With the franks, though, came a story. Mr. Ershowsky's son, or nephew, or who knows at this point, had contracted polio, and wanted more than anything else in the world to have a dog. The little boy represented half of a critical mass. The other half, I now see with the rueful wisdom of hindsight, was my father, who must have wanted more than anything else in the world to get rid of my dog. Why this was so I can't say, and why I succumbed to this second round of manipulation I cannot fathom, but I must have agreed, however reluctantly, because off my dog went once again, not to perform brave deeds on a battlefield, but to a deli, to succor a Jewish stand-in for Tiny Tim.

This began as a good-faith effort to tell a story about a cherished dog, and here I am, still trying to figure my parents out. One thing I can say about them with reasonable certainty is that they were not great dog lovers. One thing I can say about myself at that time is that I didn't fight them tooth and nail for the right to keep Mr. Fluff in our home. I don't recall weeping or screaming, or throwing a last-ditch fit. I do remember, though, the little channel between Fluffy's eyes and how smooth it felt when I ran my thumb up it; how he strutted his stuff on his squat little legs, and how he could sit at the dinner table, begging for food for hours on end.

6

SEAMUS AND SPUD

Judith Lewis Mernit

They were born in June, the year a Chinese man stood before the tanks in Tiananmen Square and the Berlin Wall gave way to perestroika. The year I got married to a man I didn't love because I didn't know what else to do.

In the first picture I took of them together, they are carrying a stick. Maybe carrying isn't the right word: They are fighting. Seamus, a cairn terrier with ears still too big for his head, has a crazed look, the whites of his eyes exposed like an Appaloosa's; Spud, a muddy-brown blur of a toy-breed mutt, holds his end of the stick so fiercely next to the other dog's clamped jaws that the force of it lifts Seamus's puny body off the ground.

The ground is mottled with turned leaves and the dim amber sunlight of a Minnesota October. I remember the dogs growling, pulling, shaking, tearing, fiercely devoted to the first in a long series of battles that would last the rest of their lives. They are each four months old.

I took the picture when I was twenty-nine. My new husband, Michael, and I had found little brown Spud and his four all-black brothers in a clear plastic pen at the store where we bought food for our cats and turtles. We set him on the floor and watched him run back and forth between us, throwing his stubby little front legs out straight with every stride, like a cartoon puppy. We paid three hundred dollars for him and brought him home, believing our landlord wouldn't notice a dog so tiny. When the landlord caught Michael sneaking Spud outside under his jacket, we found a loft apartment in downtown Saint Paul with high ceilings and a lobby that every day after work filled with yipping dogs and the singsong voices of the people who talked to them.

Now that Spud had forced us to move where dogs were legal, I saw no reason to settle for just one. I set to work combing the newspaper listings for the dog I'd wanted since I was a child surrounded by mutts and poodles. A dog that would follow me anywhere and could be trained to do tricks. A cairn terrier, like Dorothy's Toto.

I found him in the classifieds. He had been born to a family on a farm, the progeny of ratters, and Spud and I went to meet them all in a parking lot on the outskirts of town. The breeder, three little boys, and a pile of puppies spilled out of the car, and before long, one of the puppies had pinned Spud on his back. Only one hung back, and I claimed him as mine.

Seamus, as I named him on the way home, must have been sick or nervous that day, because within his first week at home, he took to standing over the water dish with his upper lip curled and an eerie rumble emitting from his puppy throat. Neither dog nor cat nor turtle dared come near. The first time I tried to move him away, he bit clear through the soft skin between my thumb and forefinger. One of our turtles died in his jaws; we hastily gave away our pet rabbits. The cats hid. Still in his puppyhood, Seamus held us captive in fear.

"You can't keep that dog," Michael would say to me. "He's vicious. He's going to hurt somebody." But it wasn't in me to give up a dog. Instead, I took him to obedience class, where I was told that my dog was too aggressive for a class setting. I tried another class, but Seamus lunged at an Airedale, and I left. Finally, I found a woman just over the border, in Wisconsin, who trained Rottweilers — Rottweilers! Big-headed dogs, powerful and skilled. I figured there was no kidding around with them. Her name was Marion, and she lived forty-five miles away. I diligently went to her beginner class once a week, which more than once required driving through a blizzard.

Both Marion and her peaceful Rottweilers found my scrappy terrier delightful. "You need to have more fun with him," she told me once, skittering her fingers around on the floor, watching him puppy-pounce among them. Obedience trainers back then had yet to come around to schooling dogs with clickers and treats, so Marion taught me to hold my dog at heel with a chain collar and praise him boisterously when he cooperated. Within weeks, Seamus had stopped growling and started to work. Within a month, he lived to work.

At his novice class graduation, he earned the title Most Improved Dog.

There's nothing like training a dog to forge a relationship with one. I will never in my life cease to marvel at the way dogs learn things — the ferocity and speed of it all, the apparent joy they take in knowing the meaning of a cue. In a world full of rebel terriers, Seamus was the rare biddable one. He learned to heel. He sat up and begged. He'd give you five, then ten; roll over, jump into my arms, fetch. He could sing — a joyful, pleasantly medium-timbre howl — on cue. His rehabilitation from snarling cur to devoted pal brought up in me a passion I had not yet felt in my life, for anything.

And yet he still gave Spud not a moment's peace. Seamus guarded everything — refrigerator, dog door, tennis ball, food, chair, cat, hat, radio, car. Anything Spud wanted to get close to, Seamus defended with a growl that would crescendo rapidly into a snapping lunge. Spud would snap and lunge back, in his bouncy little Ewok way, but he always backed off. Had we never intervened on his behalf, he might have died of thirst.

Over time, it became clear that Spud would be Michael's dog, while Seamus was mine, and the simmering war between the dogs no doubt mirrored the low hum of our marital discontent. Two years after we acquired the dogs, when I was offered a job in California, we considered splitting them up while I got settled and waited for Michael to join me. But perhaps I knew the future. In the end, I wasn't able to leave him behind. Seamus traveled to California in a crate buckled into the back seat of my Subaru Justy. Spud — for some fifteen hundred miles through Iowa and South Dakota, and through the mountain passes of Utah and the deserts of Nevada — slept in my lap.

I'd been in Los Angeles less than a month when Michael admitted an affair and I fell impossibly in love with a sports reporter. I filed for divorce.

ON THE FIRST OF JUNE, just before his seventeenth birthday, Seamus stood up in the wire crate that served as his refuge, ignored the open door, and tried to walk out through the back. He bumped his head, tried again, and finally lay down with a moan of miserable surrender. He was blind, deaf, and incontinent. I had dreaded the moment when I'd have to decide whether his life was worth living, but there was no mistaking it. The house-call vet came to the house the next day. Seamus held his last meal — a piece of cheese pizza — between his small graceful paws the way a child holds a fallen bird. After he'd chewed it to the crust, we took him inside to his favorite spot on the couch, lighted candles, and talked as the vet prepared the first needle. As the doctor's hand came close, Seamus jerked up to bite it.

Spud had remained hearty, bright-eyed, and sharp, still responding to voices, and still jumping into laps. I kept him out of the room while his lifelong adversary was silenced by the second needle, the one that stopped his heart, and when I returned, Spud was as he had always been: sitting in the toddler's lounger I'd bought for him at IKEA, panting and wagging his stubby tail, looking forward to whatever would happen next. He had never had a day of physical distress in his life — no bouts of diarrhea, no sudden limp, no kennel cough, no worms, not even a flea. I thought it was possible, after seventeen years of strife, that Spud would live out his last years in blissful, simple peace.

Oh, how little humans know of dogs and their happiness! Spud spent the first night without Seamus pattering back and forth through the rooms of the house, looking for where that other dog had gone. In the morning I found him crumpled in the spot where Seamus's kennel had been, lying in a puddle of urine. I put the crate back where it had been, and Spud went inside. He would not eat. I picked him up periodically and put him outside to relieve himself, but when he came back in, he went straight to the crate.

I fed him stinky cat food. I took him to the groomer, who adored him — he always liked to be groomed — and he cheered up for the hour he was there. But when he came home, he drooped over in my hands like a loose sack of beans.

A week and a day after Seamus had died, I asked my friend Pandora to come over and mind Spud while I went to a yoga class. A bright, sweet-smelling, gentle-voiced beauty, Pandora had always loved Spud, and he'd responded in kind; I figured a visit from her would turn him around. I left a few minutes before she arrived. As I was headed into class, she called and told me to come home.

Spud had tottered out of the crate toward her, she reported, and climbed into her lap when she sat on the floor. He looked up at her, offered a lick, and dropped his head. She considered whether to rush him to the vet, but he was already lifeless. So she simply held him quietly, and watched him die.

An hour later, at four o'clock that afternoon, I got a call from Spud's vet, who had given him a geriatric exam the week before. The results of his blood tests had come back. They showed him to be astonishingly healthy. "Just get him in here and get his teeth cleaned!" she admonished me.

"He's dead," I told her. "Spud died an hour ago."

She gasped.

He died of a broken heart.

WE MAKE A DISTINCTION between the deaths of humans and the deaths of our pets, but grief still follows the same old rules. It causes the same unraveling, provokes the same disintegration of character and beliefs. After my mother had died, I had gone to clean out the attic of the house where I'd grown up, and found a box full of flowery pastel birthday decorations, bought for a twenty-first-birthday party that never happened — I'd capriciously decided not to come home that weekend from New York, where I was attending school. The moment of clarity, and deep regret, that seized me in the wake of my two little dog companions' coincident deaths was no less sharp. I had screwed up again.

When the dogs died, I was living in a tiny apartment attached to the house of a man I'd been involved with for three years, who had made it clear to me that I was not his first choice. Nor was he mine, when I sat down to think about it. "It's for the best," he said to me as I rocked little Spud's form in my lap, paralyzed with sobs. I screamed and swore: What did he know? He didn't. Because I wasn't crying only over the loss of Spud. I was crying for what I'd just learned, and what I would continue to figure out over the next few grief-stricken months. We think love is cuddling up together on the sofa, but it's not. That's just what you do to get your body warm. Love is something altogether more fraught, and tangled up, than that. And I didn't have it.

I rode my bike around a lot in those days, talking to myself out loud, grateful for the rise of the Bluetooth headset, which now blurs the lines between the busy and the crazy. "I should have never left Minnesota," I blurted. "I should have never left my husband." I believed this at the time — not because I would have been happier had I stayed, but because it would have been better for the dogs. I could have gone on obedience-training Seamus with Marion the Rottweiler lady; I could have taken him to agility class. I could have continued living the sensible life I was cut out for and the dogs were born to, in a house with a garden and a nice fenced yard to play ball in. I should have had their teeth cleaned.

It also occurred to me during this time that I should have learned to properly groom a cairn terrier. Their hard, thick coats require regular thinnings, accomplished with a small instrument called a stripping knife and an agile flick of the wrist. I let Seamus grow shaggy and messy. I was wrong.

Most of all, though, I regretted not paying more attention to Spud. To who Spud was. I had dismissed him as vapid and silly — an intrepid little hiking buddy, but not exactly deep. And yet in the clarity that comes with death, I had to wonder: What does it take for a perfectly healthy being to lie down and die of grief in a week? If that's not depth of character, what is?

Spud was all heart. Love was all he had, all he did, and he did it well. Spud loved: cats, other dogs, baby squirrels, rabbits, children, all the people at the Silver Lake dog park. "SPUUUUUDDDD!" they'd yell as we walked in, and he'd

come bounding, with his silly, rocky, straight-legged gallop, across the park into the crowd. And he apparently loved
most of all that shaggy little dog on the other end of that
stick, the one who in those grumbles had imparted information I failed to intercept. Spud had loved Seamus, more than
I had ever loved anyone. Loved the standoffs, the mock battles, the difficult pleasure of getting to the water bowl. I was
ashamed that I had taken them for rivals.

I can't say it was an abrupt, conscious decision, that I
suddenly stopped while sweeping the floor and said to myself: "What if I die this way?" It was more a feeling that
crept over me in odd moments. On a walk through the hills
with my still-surviving dog, a pit bull named Molly, when a
sharp loneliness seized me so hard I thought my own heart
had stopped. (Molly was lovely, but she followed her own
discriminating tastes when it came to humans, and I was not,
sad to say, among the select.) It happened in front of the computer, when I'd forgo deadlines to obsessively search for
new dogs on the website of Colonel Potter's Cairn Terrier
Rescue, hoping to find a stand-in for the departed. It happened before the office vending machine, when I'd pretend
to contemplate the food products behind their battered
plastic doors while tracing back the string of events that
had brought me here. It felt less like a choice than the inevitable result of random luck, or lack of it. I pressed the but-
ton; egg salad moved out of sight, replaced with hard-boiled
eggs.

A man came around the corner, one of my coworkers,
Al, who edited the news section. "So," he said, sincerely
meaning to be funny. "Kill any more of your pets today?"

Right there, in full view of my lunching coworkers, I fell to my knees and sobbed.

THREE OF THE FIVE PEOPLE in my immediate family died young. Each left me with a sickening sense of failure I will carry with me the rest of my life. I will never have another father with whom to make belated peace. I will never have another twenty-first birthday to celebrate with Mom. My big sister and I can never put aside the respective files of sins we kept on each other. My brother and I — the survivors — now say "I love you" to each other perhaps more often than is necessary. Because you can't make up with a person who has died.

You can, however, try again with a dog. One night I had dinner with a writer friend, Susan, who has lost many dogs and keeps adopting more. "You think you've lost everything," she said to me, "but when you look into that next dog's eyes you'll know: it's all one big dog soul." That's not to say you will have the same relationship you had with the dog before, mostly because you are not who you were when that dog showed up. You will have something different.

Two weeks after Spud's death, a puppy turned up on Petfinder.com, where homeless pets from around the country line up for human suitors like prospective dates. He looked precisely like the cairn terrier who struggled with that stick so many years ago: big ears, wheat-colored coat with black ears and nose, suspicious gaze in the one dark eye that loomed out from his profile shot. The rescue people had named him Thomas and tied a red bandana around his neck to make him look sporty. You could tell it was an act.

He had, at nine months, already caused enough trouble that he got kicked out of someone's house. This appealed to me.

Seamus had been gone exactly twenty-one days when my friend Cindy and I drove ninety miles east of Los Angeles to get Thomas. He had not been house-trained and had no idea what a leash meant. He appeared to be perilously close to his wolfish, rat-hunting origins, with little interest in humans. On the way home, we stopped at Jamba Juice, and we sat outside on a little strip of mall grass, sipping our pomegranate smoothies and staring at the strange, puzzled dog, who looked around at everything but us.

Thomas turned out to be a hard one, not biddable at all, which did not release me from my do-over deal with the universe. I enrolled him in the first class available on the schedule at the West Los Angeles Obedience Training Club, and kept him there until he stopped slipping his lead to run off with the soccer players who shared the park. I trained him to take tunnels, jumps, and teeters. I took him to an Earthdog trial, where rodent-hunting terrier breeds prove their gameness by burrowing underground in search of a rat. At one of those trials, a woman with some expertise in the terrier world grabbed him away from me. "This dog needs to be stripped!" she yelled, and proceeded to school me in the art of stripping a cairn terrier.

One week at the end of August, I left Thomas at the puppy camp, where he'd fallen hard for a spindly Italian greyhound. I packed a truck full of gear, tents, and wigs and drove a thousand miles north to the Burning Man festival near Reno, Nevada. It was time to give up and start over, to find another place to live and another way to live it. I cried, danced, slept far too little, and walked until my legs ached. Late one night, I wandered out to the Temple, the place at Burning Man where people remember their loved and dead. With a Sharpie, I wrote verses in big block letters to my two little dogs. "I'm sorry," I wrote, "for not seeing you."

And with that, I began a new year. Drawing on the failed experiment of all the years that had come before, I wrote up a list of intentions — a design for a new life — and threw it into a bonfire. My wish, above all: a life full of love. I would put my foot down and settle for nothing less.

Two months later, I walked up a mountain under a full November moon with Thomas at my heels, surrounded by friends, one of whom had brought his neighbor, Billy. By the time the night was over, Billy and I had split off from the group and talked for eight hours straight. Two years later, to the day, we got married with less fuss and forethought than it takes to plan a vacation.

We do carry our sticks: our struggle over our shared desire to write something true and profound; our ideas about how to change the world; our sometimes divergent opinions about the care of the baby pit bull we adopted after Molly's death. (Never much of an animal person before, my husband has become a relentless spoiler of dogs.) I was inclined to think that meeting him was magic, but it was not: if I didn't find him before, it was because of the simple fact that none of us can recognize what we haven't already seen. In his death, Spud had shown me how to live.

7.

CALICO

Melissa Cistaro

Calico saved me. Not only from the fire but also from the constant longing I had for my mother. It was Calico that I counted on to be home every day after school as I walked down our long gravel driveway. Past the blackberry bushes, past the pink tea roses. She was always there. For eighteen years Calico was the mother cat in our big yellow house. Twenty-three kittens. Seventy-eight (at the very least) field mice, birds, and blue-bellies that she captured out in the pasture. An occasional alligator lizard and close to a dozen tailless voles. Every day, she watched us diligently with her big gold and black eyes.

The fire was an accident. It was close to three in the morning when Calico pounced on my bed and began the distinct *yee-oowl* sound that came from deep in her throat whenever she'd caught a prize out in the field. Annoyed by her loud cries, I shoved her off my bed. Sometimes she'd bring me a mouse that was still alive and then play chase with it on the borders of my quilt. Usually though, she'd crouch on the dark blue carpet, and I'd hear her crunching up tiny bones like she was eating a whole walnut shell.

But on this particular night, she pushed her nose hard against my face. Between her cries, I heard the crackling and popping coming from outside my window. I turned and saw the glow of flames twelve inches from the head of my bed. Our house was on fire.

I swept up Calico in my arms, ran to the foot of the stairs, and screamed for my dad to wake up. In a frantic scramble, my father ran to the back of the house and began to douse the fire with our garden hose. The flames were burning the outside of my bedroom walls, turning the thick yellow paint black and brittle.

The fire chief later scolded my father for leaving the pile of chemical-soaked rags outside my window, and for not having smoke detectors in the house. "You know how fast this old house would have burned down?" he asked.

My dad shook his head.

"Twenty-four minutes and there would have been nothing left," said the fire chief.

I tried to imagine what it would be like to lose everything in twenty-four minutes. I knew then that Calico must have come to my room within seconds of the fire starting.

She saved us from losing our house that night — and maybe our lives. But it wasn't just that night. Calico saved me all the time. This yearning I had for my mother was because she wasn't around much. I never knew when I would see her next. Calico was always available. Her willingness to

let me love her and just hang out with her on the brown velvet couch was the kind of closeness I needed most.

Sometimes she'd let down her guard and race wild
through the house. She got this crazy, almost-possessed look
in her wide eyes. Then she would tear around our house,
galloping full speed through every room, hitting walls and
racing upside down along the underside of my grandmother's old wing chair. She made me laugh, brought me out of
my contained self.

Calico had an odd routine with me. Every morning
she'd study me in the shower. My father had converted an
old wine barrel into an open stall but never got around to figuring out how to put a curtain around it. There was also no
doorknob on the bathroom, so Calico could push her way in.
Every shower I took, Calico would stand sentinel on the zinc
tub across from the wine barrel and watch me. Her pupils
narrowed and her eyes rarely blinked as the steam rose up
around me and filled the room. I became self-conscious of
her steady gaze on my naked body. It made me uneasy. I was
starting to develop breasts and hips, and I felt like she was
documenting the changes in me, that she quite possibly had
arrived from another planet to report on the human body.

Calico gave birth to the strangest assortment of kittens.
There were always two or three with tail issues — kinks
and knots, and sometimes no tail at all. My brothers and I
gave them silly names like Kinks One and Kinks Two and
Tommy-No-Tail. My father kept saying he was going to get
her fixed "once and for all," but he was sidetracked raising
my brothers and me, and inevitably Calico would show up
fat and moody one more time. As soon as her litter was old

enough, we'd take them down to Lucky's Market in a cardboard box with a sign that said "Free Kittens." I'd point out how unique their tails were, and that was always a good selling point.

Calico chose to have her last litter underneath my covers late one night when no one else was home. I curled myself up on my pillow to give her all the room she needed as I listened in the dark to the sounds of a mother cat giving birth and the tiny cries that followed. I lifted my quilt and watched the last wet black kitten slip out of her body and onto my pink sheets. I marveled at the way she licked each kitten dry. She cared for them with such natural confidence. How did she know how to take care of her kittens? I wanted to know. I wanted to know because I couldn't understand why it was so hard for my mom to take care of my brothers and me when we were small. And how was I ever going to learn how to be a mother?

My mom was also an animal lover, but in a different way. She collected animals — cats, chickens, sheep, goats, geese, cows. You name it, and she had one running around the property at one time or another. We picked up a curly black puppy one summer at a gas station outside the airport. Mr. Wiggly didn't live long. Most of my mom's animals didn't have particularly long lives — it was often some misfortune or an infection that waited too long before she took the animal to see the veterinarian.

I WAS TEN YEARS OLD when I went to visit my mom one summer in Washington State. She was living on a dairy farm with 180 cows and her new boyfriend, Roger Short. She was engrossed in her *New York Times* crossword puzzle at the table when I asked her if I could go down to the calf barn. She nodded her head and said that I might look for a few good chicken eggs while I was there.

The black-and-white calves shoved their heads through the wood slats of the stalls and stared at me with their big polished eyes. "Roger likes to wean them young," my mom had told me. I decided to do a little exploring around the barn. I walked past the room filled with burlap sacks of corn and grain and peeked into several empty stalls. At the end of the walkway, there were two tall white buckets with lids on them, the plastic kind that painters use. They looked out of place to me for some reason, like maybe they were set down there and forgotten. I pried the lid off the bucket closest to me.

I was not certain if what I was seeing was right or true. Kittens. Piled up to the brim. Clean white fur. Brown, black, tan, orange. Small paws with fleshy pads as soft as apricot skin. Wiry tails. Tiny pink noses. Whiskers, as fine as fishing line, almost transparent.

I pushed the lid back on. I guessed that there were more than a dozen piled up in there. I pried open the other bucket only because I wanted it to be something different. But it wasn't. One all black, one striped orange, one smoky gray, more colors underneath. Soft triangle ears, thin as potato chips. I wanted to stop staring but I couldn't. A small calico kitten was lying across the top of the heap. Its eyes were closed, but the shallow part of its belly moved — barely — up and down like it was in a deep sleep. I wanted to touch it, but I was afraid.

I ran up the hill through the wet grass and opened the screen door. My mom was at the table with her crossword puzzle, her coffee, and a cigarette.

"Why are all those kittens in the white buckets?" I asked.

She kept looking at her crossword puzzle like she was just about to figure something out.

"Oh, that," she said with a frown. "You *weren't* supposed to see that. Roger was supposed to dump them."

I waited for her to say something more.

"I'm sorry you had to see that, darlin'. It's the way of the farm here. There were just too many kittens."

"What do you mean too many?" I asked.

"Those were feral kittens, wild and inbred — just the ugly ones. Believe me. I can tell the inbred ones right away. Their eyes are wide-set and slightly askew. Their heads are oversized."

"But how did they die?"

My mom got up from the table with her ceramic coffee cup and walked into the kitchen. I could tell she didn't want to listen to my questions.

"Chloroform is what Roger said to use." She measured out a heaping spoonful of sugar into her cup. "But power-steering fluid works just as well. It's very quick. They don't suffer."

I felt my throat tighten up like a fist. My legs were as wobbly and uncertain as the calves down in the barn.

"Mom, I saw one breathing on the top, a calico one, not an ugly one, but a long-haired calico."

"There were no calicos," she said. "And you did *not* see any kittens breathing."

"I did Mom, I definitely saw that one on top."

She slammed the garbage can lid down.

"None of those kittens were breathing, you understand?"

I was strangely afraid of her. She knew how much I loved kittens. I tried to stop the image of her hands pushing those kittens into the white buckets. But I knew there was a calico. I knew that she killed them.

WHEN I RETURNED HOME, Calico was curled up on my bed. I sat down beside her and ran my fingers through the thick white patch of fur on her chest. There was nowhere else I wanted to be. I would no longer confide in my mom, but I could talk to Calico. She listened to everything. She was like me. She could keep secrets.

As the years passed, I'd tell her about the things I was afraid of and ashamed of — like getting drunk and high in eighth grade and lying to my dad about where I was going on the weekends. I also learned from Calico how to sneak back into the house late at night. I had watched her out in the field so many times that I knew exactly how to take those silent and slow, slow, stalking steps.

Shortly after I graduated from high school, my father got into a huge financial mess and our yellow house had to be sold. Close to everything in our house was auctioned off on the front porch in four and a half hours. My dad explained to me that it might be best for Calico to stay with the house, where she had spent her whole life. She had become such a part of the house and the land there. The new owners of our house agreed to sign a "cat clause" stating that they would keep Calico as long as we wanted — that we could come get her anytime. But my brothers and my father and I scattered like wildflower seeds after we lost the house. I don't think any of us really knew where we were headed. No one had a place suitable for Calico, who had slowed down considerably but still loved to hunt out in the field.

I pushed the guilt of leaving Calico as far down as it would go.

I had to believe that my dad was right, that she was meant to stay behind. How could I have left Calico? I now ask myself. I was eighteen and trying to figure out who I was. I somehow believed that, when I figured it all out, I would have the perfect place for Calico to live out her last days. A backyard with a field of tall grass, sunshine, and lizards.

I was living in Los Angeles and going to UCLA when my dad called to let me know Calico had died. I was rushing off to a midterm in my art history class and couldn't take the information in properly. I suppose I didn't want to take in the news at all, because I went on for a few days not thinking about Calico. I woke up one morning four days later, and I could have sworn I was sleeping in the brass bed I had slept in while growing up. I reached up to twist one of the brass knobs that was always loose, and found nothing. Then I caught the scent of a rubbery beige flea collar and the smell of Calico's black and tan fur. It was unmistakably Calico's scent that filled the room. I missed her terribly.

Until that moment, I had not cried over Calico. The loss had been lying dormant inside me. It was my pattern to go underground, where it is silent, and to keep my secrets and feelings safely tucked away. My best childhood friend has told me that I was always like a cat — the observer, the quiet thinker, the one who sits at the top of stairs and listens. But it was Calico who taught me to also be fearless. To run with wild abandon when the urge struck. To be grateful for mice tails and blue-belly lizards. To sit quietly in a window filled with sunlight. To be generous with leftover cereal milk. To stand naked and unflinching while being watched.

Perhaps it is the steadiness of an animal's presence that gives us comfort. Calico, a black, white, and tan cat, provided that steadiness for me. People could be unreliable. People could leave. But Calico stayed for eighteen years. I have to believe she had a purpose here, and it wasn't to report back to another planet on the naked human body. She was the mother who stayed. And although I hid my grief when she left, she surfaces so often now when I write. She is within arm's reach across the table. I can feel the stretch of her spine against the palm of my hand. She keeps showing up to tell me more. It is her indelible spirit that begs me to keep her alive for as long as I can here on the page.

8.

RED THE PIG

May-lee Chai

Growing up on a farm, I wasn't a fool. I knew our animals were destined to become food. But the year I raised my pig, I hadn't expected to be the instrument of his death. Red wasn't even supposed to be mine to begin with.

"Pigs are 'farm savers,'" my brother insisted one night at dinner. "Everyone knows that."

"We don't need any more animals," I said, thinking of our seven hundred laying hens, two Holsteins, and three goats. I was seventeen and in my last year of high school, and I wanted no part in raising pigs.

"Please, Mom. Please," my brother begged. "We'll just raise bottle pigs. You feed 'em until they're big enough to survive on their own, then you sell 'em. Jimmy knows all about it." (Not his real name.)

"Jimmy's not going to be doing the work," I argued.

"Sure he will! He promised. He's gonna help me. Please, Mom. Can we get a sow?"

My mother's brow wrinkled. Ever since we had moved to this town from the East Coast, we'd had trouble fitting in. My father was Chinese, my mother white. People in our town weren't used to seeing this kind of mixed-race family, and they'd told my brother and me to our faces that we were the Devil's Spawn. God didn't want the races to mix, that's why he put them on different continents.

My mother had tried hard to find a way for my younger brother to fit in, be accepted in a community where masculinity was defined by how many acres your family owned and farmed, by how many head of cattle you raised, and — unspoken by any of us but secretly acknowledged — by the color of your hair and eyes. Straw hair, blue eyes, trumped my brother every time.

Our father was working as a consultant, having left the teaching job that had brought us to this small community in South Dakota. He traveled constantly. That was a factor too. Boys in this town grew up knowing exactly where their fathers were, in the fields, in the barns, or in the local bar.

Hence our growing menagerie. Each addition was an attempt by my mother to find the right combination of animals that would help my brother to belong. And if the animals kept me busy too, my parents figured, then all the better.

"I'll ask around," she said finally.

My brother turned to give me a triumphant smile.

And so in August, our newly acquired sow went into labor.

My brother and his friend were pulling the piglets from the grunting sow's uterus. My brother cleared the gunk off their faces and placed them near their mother's teats. When the placenta was finally expelled, he gave it to the sow to eat.

The sow had given birth to eleven piglets. More than expected.

"These'll bring in good money," my brother crowed.

I watched the helpless, tiny piglets grunting at their mother's belly. They were cold despite the August heat and nestled closer to her for warmth. There was barely space for them all, and they tumbled over each other, snorting, their eyes closed tight. Despite myself, I had to laugh at their antics.

"Here, May-lee. Hold one." And my brother put a piglet in my hand.

It was warm and squiggly, unable to hold still, only slightly longer than my hand, but heavier than I'd expected.

"They're cute," I admitted.

Then my brother went to the pump to wash the afterbirth and blood from his arms.

The next day at dawn, I went out to do the morning chores with my brother as usual. The best thing about August was that the early mornings were still light but not as hot as July. Soon enough we'd be rising before the sun, and the mornings would be growing cooler, then cold, then bitter cold. But late summer was a perfect time of year. And for the first time in a long time, my brother seemed happy as we headed into the barn.

The piglets were nestled up to the sow's teats, pulling frantically. Then the sow stood up, all four hundred pounds rising faster than I would've thought possible. The piglets dropped off, squeaking, and she shook her head, flapping her long ears. She trotted off to the far side of the barn to poop, leaving her piglets to huddle together, crying for her piteously. Then we saw them. Three piglets squashed flat on the concrete floor. Their mother must have rolled over on them during the night.

"Wow," I said.

"She probably didn't know they were there behind her. They probably couldn't fit on the other side." My brother was trying to sound tough, trying to sound like a farmer, but I could tell he was sad. He was the animal lover, not me. Now he grabbed a shovel. "They must have died instantly."

"You'd think." I turned away to start watering the chickens. I didn't want to watch him scrape the piglets' bodies from the floor.

By that afternoon there were more problems.

The sow couldn't drop her milk. We visited the veterinarian, who diagnosed mastitis and sold us syringes and oxytocin. "That should do the trick," he said.

But it didn't. Two days later she still couldn't nurse. The piglets were visibly thinner. They squealed pitiably. A few tried to stand, but fell over, their heads too heavy for their ever-weakening legs.

By day three, the vet paid a call. It was worse than we thought. He recognized the sow when my brother said where he'd bought her. She was a dry sow, meaning she had incurable mastitis. She was unable to nurse her piglets.

My mother and I drove to the grain elevator and bought bags of Purina Pig Milk, chocolate-flavored formula for piglets, as well as giant plastic bottles and plastic nipples from the farm supply store. My brother and I mixed the formula, but most of the piglets were too weak to drink. We sat on the floor of the barn, piglets in our laps, dribbling the chocolate milk across their tongues, trying to encourage them to suckle.

By the end of the week, all but four of the piglets were dead. We sold the sow to pay for the vet bills and formula, all these added expenses my brother hadn't anticipated. His friend, the self-proclaimed pig expert, suddenly bowed out of the whole project, announcing his parents wanted him to run his own night crawler business out of their garage instead. And my brother, perhaps overtired from spending all his days and nights watching over the dying piglets, came down with a fever. He was bedridden now.

My brother begged me from his bed to take care of them. His room was right across the hall from mine, and even though I tried to ignore him, pretend I couldn't hear his raspy voice, he called to me, "Please, May-lee. Don't let them die."

And so I became the caretaker of my brother's piglets.

I got used to mixing their formula after I'd fed and watered the chickens, the Holsteins, and goats. I crouched in the barn and held the piglets on my knee. They nudged each other, fighting to see who could feed first. I tried feeding two at a time, but when one pulled loose and sneezed, she spat up chocolate all over my overalls.

I didn't want to grow fond of these creatures. They were too fragile. The deaths of the seven others had shown me that. So I came to think of the pigs by their colors: Red, Spotted, Pinky, and Pink Lady (after the characters in *Grease*).

They were non-names, I convinced myself. I wouldn't care about these pigs. They weren't even mine, after all.

Red grew the fastest. Soon he didn't want me to hold him. He was sturdy on his own four legs. He slurped down his milk, hiccupped, and trotted off, flapping his ears.

I had my mother take my senior picture with him for the yearbook. Red didn't like posing, and squealed and bucked in my arms. I felt as though I were trying to hold a Pacific salmon. But my mother got one good shot. I'm smiling, and Red is in focus, ears stiff and alert, matching my braids.

That fall the pigs became my full responsibility. After his illness, my brother grew depressed. The pigs were costing more than his friend had predicted; they were more like farm sinkers than savers. My brother no longer came into the barn but worked outside instead, moving the cows' grazing areas, checking the fencing, brooding.

Me, I watched the pigs grow up. There's a saying that pigs are smarter than dogs, but I found that stereotype didn't do either pigs or dogs justice. Pigs are different from dogs. These four had their own unique traits, their own way of interacting with the world — and me. To compare them to dogs would be to reduce their porcine personalities.

For example, if our dogs grew bored, they barked ceaselessly, trying to get our attention. When the pigs wanted entertainment, they waited for no one.

One Sunday after church I was making lunch with my mother when I heard a strange honking noise, almost like geese. Extremely large geese. "The pigs are out!" My mother pointed at the window.

Indeed, the pigs had busted out of the barn and were now digging across the lawn with their powerful snouts, churning up the soil. Within minutes, they'd managed to dig a trench more than two feet deep.

I threw on my coat and ran outside.

"Pigs! Pigs!" I shouted, realizing that maybe it had been a bad idea not to name them. Then I tried snorting at them, honking from the depths of my throat, which is closer to the sound pigs make than *oink, oink*! Believe me.

Red looked up, flapped his ears, ran toward me, nuzzled my jeans with his snout, then happily returned to destroying the lawn.

I ran to the barn and grabbed a metal bucket, filled it with corn.

Clanging on the bucket with the grain scoop, I shouted, "Corn! Food! Corn!" Only then was I able to lure them back to the barn, walking backward, letting Red — the leader — sniff the corn every now and then, but not allowing him to eat until I got them inside.

At least this stereotype was true: pigs really did like to hog their food.

By the time snows blanketed our farm, and the wind-chill was well below zero, the pigs no longer wanted to go outside. They were content to play in the barn, eating rapidly, then shooting their empty metal feed dishes with their snouts across the concrete floor like hockey pucks. They were growing fast, and if I wasn't careful, they could easily knock me over. Red tried to include me in their game, whacking a feed dish against my leg so hard that I had bruises for a month. After that, I learned to keep my distance while they played.

I liked to climb the vertical ladder to our loft, where we kept the Holsteins' bales of alfalfa. I sat with my legs dangling down, watching them. The pigs resembled small whales from above, I thought. They even seemed to move as if in a pod.

Of all the animals I fed, the pigs were the only ones who appeared to look at me, really notice me. Red genuinely liked to rub up against me. He seemed grateful for the food and fresh water I brought him. Even my family didn't show me as much gratitude.

My mother told me God could see me working hard, and that I would be rewarded in heaven. I loved my mother dearly, but her words weren't much consolation. Farm work was hard, I was tired, and my back ached day and night.

However, the pigs always grunted in joy when I opened the barn doors, carrying a fresh bucket of water for them. They seemed pleased after I scraped up their poop with a snow shovel and took it out of the barn. Unlike the chickens or cows, who treated me like a slow waiter, the pigs jumped up at my very appearance, happy that I had come to feed them no matter how terrible the weather outside.

By February, they were as tall as my hipbones, and heavy. When I brought them their corn and they pressed up against me, I felt genuine fear. Red's affectionate nudges could knock me over. He didn't know his own strength, but I knew the pigs could crush me now, as easily as their mother had crushed their siblings, should I lose my footing and fall in their path.

At dinner, I mentioned to my brother sadly that it might be time to sell them to a real hog farm. "They seem big enough. They're up to my hips."

"They can't have grown that fast," my brother said.

But the next morning he came out to the barn to check. "Holy!" he said. "How'd they get so big?"

"It's been six months."

"I'll get Jimmy to come up this weekend," my brother said. "We can use his pickup to take them to market. He'll know how to sell them to a hog farm."

That weekend, Jimmy showed up late, midafternoon, and he insisted on parking near the road so his pickup wouldn't get muddy, as it would if he pulled up closer to the barn. He wanted to *herd* the pigs to his truck, he said.

"That's not gonna work," I said.

But Jimmy laughed at me, a *girl* trying to tell them what to do, and my brother laughed too because he wanted a friend.

I wanted no part of this disaster. They weren't even my pigs, I told myself, so I turned my back and started walking through the snowdrifts back to our house.

Behind me, I could hear the barn doors sliding open and the squealing of the pigs. Then more squealing. Swearing from Jimmy, from my brother.

I turned around and saw the pigs taking off through the grove, heading behind the barn, running everywhere in the snow except toward the pickup truck.

"No!" I shouted. "They'll catch cold and get sick!"

Jimmy was smiling, his fallback reaction when things went wrong.

"Goddammit!" I swore, running back to the barn to fill the feeders. Then I brought out a bucket of corn. Red ran past me into the barn. His instincts were good, and he was seeking familiar shelter. Spotted and Pink Lady followed Red.

But Pinky was missing. My brother and I found her behind the barn, lying on her side in a snowdrift, panting heavily, her eyes wild. She didn't even try to sniff the corn in my bucket. I knelt down beside her. "It's okay," I said. I tried to offer her a handful of corn.

"Pigs'll get pneumonia in this weather," my brother said.

"Ya think?" I was furious. "Jimmy's an idiot. You know that, right?"

"Yeah," he said, sadly.

"You back the truck up and set up the ramp at the barn door, and I'll get them into the truck. Okay?"

"Okay," my brother said. And he walked off.

Pinky calmed down and started sniffing the corn in the bucket. She followed me to the barn.

The other pigs were agitated. Red was running back and forth. I brought them a fresh bucket of water from the pump outside.

I could hear the pickup truck coming up the gravel, but the pigs were calming now. Everything was familiar; I was there, feeding them. What was there to fear?

I'd have to trick them to get them into that truck now. I'd have to get them to trust me. One last time.

Red was guzzling water. He was not used to exercise, certainly not used to running through snow. He panted heavily.

My brother knocked on the door, but the smell of exhaust filling the barn had already warned me the truck was in place.

I filled another bucket with corn.

"You guys hungry?" I kept my voice light. I grunted at the pigs in my best pig voice. Red trotted over to me, then put his snout in the bucket. Pigs' fatal flaw is their appetite.

"Okay. Let's go," I said, and I pulled open the barn doors. My brother let down the ramp and I ducked under the topper and climbed up into the bed of the pickup, leading Red with the bucket of corn. Maybe he thought this was a new game. Why not? He had no reason not to trust me.

The other pigs followed him. Then my brother closed the pickup's back door and I jumped out the window, which he then closed before the pigs tried to follow suit.

"Those pigs aren't feeders anymore. They're market weight," Jimmy announced, coming round the side. "Bet you'll get a good price."

"Fuck you," I said, and I walked back to the house.

Indeed, when my brother returned from the stockyards in Sioux City, Iowa, that evening, he reported the pigs were more than two hundred pounds a piece. He'd been able to sell them straight for slaughter, no middleman needed.

I sat at the kitchen table. There was nothing to say. I knew the pigs had been destined to die some day. They were pork. But it didn't feel good having led my Red to his own slaughter. The only thing worse would have been to let my brother's friend continue to ineptly chase the pigs through the snow, until they fell, got sick, were injured, or died of a heart attack from the exertion.

There was no point being squeamish on a farm, I told myself.

But then I went to my room, slammed the door, and cried.

I wanted to believe I'd done the right thing, that I'd given my pig some joy while he was alive. But I wondered, when he reached the slaughterhouse did he figure out that I had betrayed him? Did he blame me? Or did he still hope that I might show up and save him in the moments before his terrifying and undoubtedly painful death?

I knew then that I could never come back to this farm. Once I left home for college, I'd have to find a place for me in the world where I could be happy, where my work would be appreciated, and where my values would be shared. I loved my family, but I never wanted to live on a farm again.

9.

THIS DOG'S LIFE

Anne Lamott

Having a good dog is the closest some of us will ever come to knowing the direct love of a mother, or God, so it's no wonder it knocked the stuffing out of Sam and me when Sadie died. I promised Sam we'd get another puppy someday, but privately I resolved to never get another dog. I didn't want to hurt that much again, if I could possibly avoid it. And I didn't want my child's heart and life to break like that again. But you don't always get what you want; you get what you get. This is a real problem for me. You want to protect your child from pain, and what you get instead is life, and grace; and though theologians insist that grace is freely given, the truth is that sometimes you pay for it through the nose. And you can't pay your child's way.

We should never have gotten a dog to begin with — they all die. While it is subversive when artists make art that will pass away in the fullness of time, or later that day, it's not as ennobling when your heart breaks.

When Sam was two, and George Herbert Walker Bush was president, I noticed I was depressed and afraid a lot of the time. I figured that I needed to move, to marry an armed man, or to find a violent but well-behaved dog. I was determined, as I am now, to stay and fight, and the men I tended to love were not remotely well enough to carry guns, so I was stuck with the dog idea.

For a while I called people who were advertising dogs in the local paper. All of them said they had the perfect dog, but perfect for whom? Quentin Tarantino? One dog we auditioned belonged to a woman who said the dog adored children, but it lunged at Sam, snarling. Other dogs snapped at us. One ran to hide, peeing as she ran. I took the initiative and placed an ad for a mellow, low-energy guard dog, and soon got a call from a woman who said she had just the dog.

As it turned out, she did have a great dog, a gorgeous two-year-old named Sadie, half black Lab, half golden retriever. Sadie looked like a black Irish setter. I always told people she was like Jesus in a black fur coat, or Audrey Hepburn in Blackglama, elegant and loving and silly. Such a lady.

Sadie was shy at first. The vet said she might have been abused as a puppy, because she acted worried about not pleasing us. He taught us how to get on the floor with her and plow into her slowly, so that she would see that we meant her no harm — that we were, in fact, playing with her. She tried to look nonchalant, but you could see she was alarmed. She was so eager to please, though, that she learned to play, politely.

Sadie lived with us for more than ten years, and saw us through great joy and great losses. She consoled us through friends' illnesses, through the deaths of Sam's grandparents. She and I walked Sam to school every day. She was mother, dad, psych nurse. She helped me survive my boyfriends and the sometimes metallic, percussive loneliness in between them. She helped Sam survive his first mean girlfriend. She'd let my mother stroke her head forever. She taught comfort.

But when she was about to turn thirteen, she developed lymphoma. The nodes in her neck were the size of golf balls. The vet said she would live a month if we didn't treat her. Part of me wanted to let her die, so we could get it over with, have the pain behind us. But Sam and I talked it over, and decided she would have half a dose of chemo: we wanted her to have one more good spring. She was better two days after the chemo. She must have had a great capacity for healing: she went in and out of remission for two years. Toward the end, when she got sick again and probably wasn't going to get well, the vet said he would walk us through her death. He said that even when a being is extremely sick, ninety-five percent of that being is still healthy and well — it's just that the other five percent feels so shitty. We would focus on the parts that were well, he said, the parts that brought her pleasure, like walks, being stroked, smelling things, and us.

Our vet does not like to put animals to sleep unless they are suffering, and Sadie did not seem to be in pain. He said that one day she would go under a bed and not come out, and when she did, he would give us sedatives to help her stay calm. One day she crawled under my bed, just as he said she would.

It was a cool, dark cave under my bed, with a soft moss-green carpet. Sadie's breathing was labored. She looked apologetic.

I called the vet and asked if I should bring her in. He said she'd feel safer dying at home, with me, but I should come in to pick up the narcotics. He gave me three syringes full. I took them under the bed with me, along with the telephone, with the ringer off, and I thought about injecting them all into my arm so my heart would not hurt so much. I wonder whether this would be considered a relapse by the more rigid members of the recovery community. I lay beside Sadie and assured her that she was a good dog even though she could no longer take care of us. I prayed for her to die quickly and without pain, for her sake, but mostly because I wanted her to die before Sam got home from school. I didn't want him to see her dead body. She hung on. I gave her morphine, prayed, talked to her softly, and called the vet. He had me put the phone beside her head, and listened for a moment.

"She's really not in distress," he assured me. "This is hard work, like labor. And she has you, Jesus, and narcotics. We should all be so lucky."

I stayed beside her on the carpet under the bed. At one point Sadie raised her head to gaze around, looking like a black horse. Then she sighed, laid her head down, and died.

I couldn't believe that she was gone, even though she'd been sick for so long. I could feel that something huge, a tide, had washed in, and then washed out.

I cried and cried, and called my brother and sister-in-law. Jamie said Stevo wasn't home, but she would leave him a note and come right over. I prayed again for my brother to be there before Sam came home from school, so he could take Sadie's body away, to spare Sam, to spare me from Sam's loss.

I kept looking at the clock. School would be out in half an hour.

Jamie and their dog, Sasha, arrived seventeen minutes after Sadie died. I had pulled the carpet out from under the bed. Sadie looked as beautiful as ever. Jamie and I sat on the floor nearby. Sasha is a small white dog with tea-colored stains; she has perky ears and tender eyes and a bright, dancing quality — we call her the Czechoslovakian circus terrier — and we couldn't resist her charm. She licked us and ran up to Sadie and licked her, too, on her face. Then she ran back to us, as if to say, "I am life, and I am here! And my ears are up at this hilarious angle!"

Stevo finally arrived, only a few minutes before Sam was usually home from school. I wanted my brother to hurry and put Sadie in the car, but it was too horrible to think that Sam might catch him sneaking Sadie out like a burglar stealing our TV. So I breathed miserably, and prayed to be up to the task. Steve sat beside Jamie. Then Sam arrived home and found us. He cried out sharply and sat on my bed alone, above Sadie. His eyes were red, but after a while Sasha made him laugh. She kept running over to the dead, exquisitely boneless mountain of majestic glossy black dog in repose on the rug. And she leaped on the bed to kiss Sam, before tending to the rest of us, like a doctor making her rounds.

Soon things got wild: My friend Neshama came over, and sat down beside me. I had called her with the news. Then a friend of Sam's stopped by, with his father, who slipped behind Sam on the bed like a shadow. The doorbell rang again, and it was another friend of Sam's, just passing by, out of the blue, if you believe in out of the blue, which I don't; and then a kid who lives up the hill came to borrow Sam's bike. He stayed, too. It was like the stateroom scene in *A Night at the Opera*. There were five adults, four kids, one white Czechoslovakian circus terrier, and one large dead black dog.

Sadie looked like an island of dog, and we looked like flotsam that had formed a ring around her. Life, death, dogs — something in us was trying to hold something together that doesn't hold together, but then does, miraculously, for the time being.

Sometimes we were self-consciously quiet, as if we were on the floor in kindergarten, and should stretch out and nap, but the teacher had gone out, so we waited.

The boys eventually went downstairs and turned on loud rock 'n' roll. The grown-ups stayed a while longer. I got a bag of chocolates from the kitchen, and we ate them, as if raising a toast. As Sadie grew deader and emptier, we could see that it was no longer Sadie in there. She wasn't going to move or change, except to get worse and start smelling. So Stevo carried her on the rolled-up carpet out to my van. It was so clumsy, and so sweet, this ungainly car-size package, Sadie's barge, and sarcophagus.

We could hear the phantom sounds of Sadie for days — the nails on wood, the tail, the panting. Sam was alternately distant and clingy and mean, because I am the primary person he banks on and bangs on. I stayed close enough so he could push me away. Sadie slowly floated off.

Then, out of the so-called blue again, six months later, some friends gave us a five-month-old puppy, Lily. She's a Rottweiler/Shar-Pei/shepherd, huge, sweet, and well behaved — mostly. She's not a stunning bathing beauty like Sadie. But she's lovely and loving, and we adore her. It still hurts sometimes, to have lost Sadie, though. She was like the floating garlands the sculptor Andy Goldsworthy made in the documentary *Rivers and Tides*: yellow and red and green leaves, connected one to another with thorns, floating away in the current, swirling, drifting back toward the shore, getting cornered in eddies, drifting free again. All along you know that they will disperse once they're out of your vision, but they will never be gone entirely, because you saw them. The leaves show you how water is like the wind, because they do what streamers do in a breeze. The garlands are a translation of this material; autumn leaves, transposed to water, still flutter.

10.

TRUE LOVE

Samantha Dunn

If wishes were horses then beggars would ride.

Where to put Gabe was our most immediate problem when we ended up at Lot no. 78 in the Enchanted Hills Mobile Home Park.

Gabe — and I say this without trace of hyperbole or hint of exaggeration — was one of the most beautiful geldings ever to bear hoof upon the earth. I see him again each time I go to a movie theater and the logo for TriStar Pictures appears on the screen — the strong white chest, the thundering legs, the wings of Pegasus spreading across the darkness, illuminating each person's face for a moment. Gabe too was pure white, and built like he could carry the world yet still take flight. Because of his Arabian dam, Gabe had a finer nose, and his eyes were rounder, blacker globes. The pink-and-gray speckled skin of his muzzle showed his Appaloosa side, but apart from those small differences he could have been that Pegasus. The fact that his name was Gabriel never felt like coincidence, archangel of the Annunciation, bringer of new order, of mercy and redemption for those who responded to him. Our love for our Gabriel was the only point of total agreement my mother, grandmother, and I ever shared.

I will write about him many times in my eventual career, and I will once receive a dismissive note from an editor at a New York publishing house going over one of my essays, incredulous that it was possible for me to own a horse if we indeed lived in a trailer park. Oh, Tiffany-Buffy-Madison of the hunt club ponies and the show horse circuit, of the Connecticut address and the Seven Sisters education, three words made it possible: Sacrifice. Determination. Delusion.

MOM WAS ALWAYS ADEPT at securing me free or cheap horses, owing to the confidence with which she said everything. She had a Scotch-and-cigarette voice, wore black cowboy boots, and could raise her eyebrows independently of each other. She was tall, big boned, and wore her extravagant auburn hair long, and then later in a wavy cap around her face. She bore only two expressions normally, either anger or amusement, as if she were perpetually getting a big joke going over everybody else's head.

The way I remember it, a friend of a friend in Santa Fe had this beautiful white horse she was afraid to ride; he shied, he bolted, he was too much of a handful. "My kid can ride him. She can ride almost anything," Mom told the woman.

She exaggerated, of course. I have never been that talented a rider, but I am tenacious, thanks in no small part to Mom setting me back up on a young bay who had run away with me when I was only seven years old. I was too young to ride that horse, and that horse was too young to be ridden by anyone, so I don't remember how the circumstance happened in the first place. But there I'd been, shaking and crying after someone grabbed the reins of the runaway bay. Mom was at my side and put her arms around me for a moment, then was telling me I was OK and to goddamn get back up there. It was scarier for me to look into the disappointment on her face than to return to the saddle, so that's what I did.

Anyway, Mom assured the woman with the white horse that I could ride. We would give him a good home and pay her a hundred dollars when we could, as I needed a new mount right away. A gray Arabian gelding she'd procured for me — a mean son of a bitch prone to biting and kicking that she'd gotten from the estate of some doctor who'd been her "friend" — I didn't ask questions — had died suddenly of a brain aneurism. Right away I fell for another horse, a lanky buckskin named Sunny owned by a cowboy in Santa Fe, but we hadn't been able to come up with the five hundred dollars to buy him, so off he went to a ranch near Clovis. It was my first real heartbreak; I cried for a good two days after seeing his black tail hanging out the end of a trailer on its way south.

My fickle heart recovered the instant I saw Gabe, before I even put my foot in the stirrup. It didn't matter that he sidestepped and tossed his head, bolted like a sidewinder and had the power to whiplash the neck of any timid rider. Whatever had made him that way, I understood. I knew that kind of anger; I was at home with it. In exchange for my understanding, he gave me his beauty when I rode him, he gave me power to move freely, and it seemed that his arched neck and even gait conferred on my family a kind of nobleness, a respectability, that was otherwise hard for a single mother, an aging grandmother, and a young girl to come by on their own.

Man's best friend may be the dog, but for a girl such as myself, the horse is not only best friend but also protector and confidant. I rode Gabe so much, so far, that I came to believe my heartbeat was the sound of his hooves. I rode him as if we were running for our lives, until he was so tired his head hung like a dog's, and then I would get off and walk beside him for miles into the open horizon of the New Mexico llano. I swam with him in lakes. One time I rode him in a relay race at a gymkhana and the saddle slipped at a full gallop. I was knocked out, a tangling rag doll underneath him as the herd of other riders thundered around us, but he stood stock-still, not daring to lift a hoof. He was still standing still, muscles quivering, when people reached me. Gabriel, angel of mercy.

MOM HAD ALWAYS MANAGED to pay for board at various stables and for riding lessons for me with a former rodeo queen named Kathy, who told me Gabe's only problem was that he'd kill himself trying to please me. Mom even paid for my membership in the Santa Fe Junior Horseman's Association, and the occasional entry into a local horse show, so that Gabe and I could run the barrels or vie for a ribbon in pole bending. Mom could pay for this only because she never bought clothes for herself, had my grandmother cut and dye her hair, manicured her own nails, said yes to every double shift and any chance at overtime, and took payouts rather than vacation days. She seemed to know instinctively which bills could be paid late or totally ignored, and she was also the kind of woman men called "saucy." A knowing laugh, a smart retort, a dirty joke delivered with impeccable timing — these made for their own currency and could buy another week or a month of nonpayment, or sometimes get things thrown in altogether for free.

But by the time we made it to the Enchanted Hills Mobile Home Park, it seemed to me something had extinguished her ability to conjure. She had quit wearing makeup, her deep-set green eyes seeming small and no longer so cat-like without the deft application of mascara and eyeliner. She had gained so much weight her polyester pants pulled across her rounded stomach and hips. Bad credit might have been the reason we arrived at Lot no. 78, but it was also a problem in finding a place to stable our Gabe, and so Mom ended up striking a deal with some guy across the road from the trailer park who had a few horses in a dirt corral with a sheet-metal lean-to for shelter and two old bathtubs for water troughs. The guy said he'd feed Gabe along with his small herd if we just supplied the hay. Deal.

I rode Gabe the few miles from the place he had been pastured to this corral as Mom dropped off some bales of alfalfa. While I hugged Gabe around the neck, she put my saddle in the station wagon. Around us, chickens scratched at the dirt. A rusting car fender and some old bald tires littered one corner of the corral.

"We'll figure something out," she told me. I continued to hug his white neck and felt the warmth of his breath as he nuzzled my side.

"This is only temporary. C'mon. Sam, damn it. C'mon." Mom sounded annoyed. She always sounded annoyed.

THE NEXT PART I BLAME ON MYSELF.

I was busy with school, the weather turned rainy for a few days, I tried out for the track team and, because the coach needed "big" girls for the shot put and discus, I got in — even though I couldn't run fast enough to save myself from a burning building if I had to.

What I'm trying to say is that two weeks went by before I went to the corral to check on Gabe. Mom always worked and Gram didn't drive, and besides, the deal was that if I wanted a horse I had to take care of him. The guy who owned the place was feeding him, I reasoned, so Gabe could get by without his usual grain and carrots and grooming for a couple weeks. We'd all had to get by, make do; this was Gabe's part. Besides, he'd probably even be happy for some time off from our long rides.

I got up on Saturday morning to walk the good mile it was through the trailer park, over the old highway, and down the road to the corral with Gabe's bridle slung over my shoulder like a purse and carrots stuck in the back pocket of my jeans. When I got there, it took a moment for my brain to understand what my eyes were seeing, to even recognize my own horse.

Standing head down in a corner with his hind leg cocked was Gabe, or what had to be Gabe, but I could see the ribs on this white horse, his hide bloodied from the kicks and bites of the other horses. Tangles pulled at his mane and a piece of baling wire snarled the end of his tail.

"Gabe!" I yelled, climbing over the aluminum gate and running to him. He lifted his head for a moment then looked down, as if embarrassed, not walking toward me.

I threw my arms around him, feeling his bones, seeing the eye sockets sunken from dehydration. If any food or water had come his way in these two weeks, it had been by chance. I felt the pain of guilt like a smack to the face, which made me want to either cry or kill something. Luckily at that moment the guy who had made the arrangement with Mom came out of his grubby adobe, saving me from having to cry.

I think this is what happened: I think I turned on him the way women in my family are known to do, with shoulders back and teeth bared, my body drawn to the fullness of its five feet eight inches, a flood of the most vile Spanish words ever known to a white girl spewing from my mouth.

"*¿Que estas haciendo, carbon? ¡Pinche puto!* Have you looked at this horse lately? Have you, *pendejo*, have you?" I am pretty sure I screamed at him. He stood with his hands on the hips of his dirty jeans, not wearing a belt, his face red but his shoulders shrugging.

"Don't be talking to me like that!" I vaguely remember a scruff of gray beard and mustache hiding what must have been surprise on his face. "Your momma don't pay me nothing. I was doing her a favor — "

"Oh, just *callate*, you stupid asshole." Respect for my elders was never a concept well taught to me. I slipped Gabe's bridle over his head and started to lead him from the corral, my look daring the guy to say anything else.

He shook his head and turned away.

GRAM PUT HER HAND ON THE SPLINTERY RAILING of the porch as if to steady herself. "Well, Christ Almighty." She looked back over her shoulder and yelled to the door. "Deanne! Come see this! Dee! For god's sake!"

I'd put a halter on Gabe and had looped the lead rope through the chain link in front of the trailer, crying now as I picked up the brushes from the grooming box I'd pulled from the shed.

Gram reached out to run her hand down the length of Gabe's head, murmuring there, boy, easy, boy, as she did. She bent and kissed his muzzle, leaving a red bow from her lipstick in the center between his nostrils. She knew how to touch a horse, her fingers expert and reassuring. Growing up on Yankee Bush in rural Pennsylvania, she had never known life without horses. The way she told it, she was riding a pony named Buster as soon as she could walk, and then later her grandfather's saddlebred, Belle. As an adult she would have Salty and Becky and Captain, an iron-mouthed Morgan purchased for my grandfather that he never could ride successfully. Gram never rode now; in fact, I hadn't ever seen her on a horse except in the old black-and-white photos stashed in the cedar chest, but I never doubted she was a horsewoman.

"Sammy, go get some carrots from the fridge, and get my shampoo and conditioner from under the vanity." She didn't take her eyes off Gabe as she spoke.

I didn't say anything as I headed into the trailer, passing my mom in the kitchen as I went to the bathroom to find the Breck shampoo and conditioner Gram always used. I could hear the loud bellow of Mom's voice outside and Gram's sharp nattering that followed, the two going on like that for some minutes. I didn't need to hear the words, because I knew the tone, so I stayed in the bathroom and thought about what a bad person I had been to let Gabe suffer. Gabe, the only totally good thing I had ever known. I sat on the edge of the bathtub and hit my thighs with my fists, but no matter how hard I hit I could not hurt myself the way I thought I deserved.

I seem to remember hearing Mom on the phone after a time, her voice shaken slightly, absent the usual resonant swagger. I think she was talking to Fred, our farrier and a sheriff's deputy. I think she said, "I need your help."

By the time the sun was leaving a terra-cotta trail across the horizon, Fred and his brother, and maybe a few other off-duty deputies, had strung some barbed wire across the open section in the otherwise fenced couple acres next to the trailer park. Mom had found the land's owner, managed to talk him into leasing the pasture, and prevailed on Fred's good nature to spend his one day off putting in a fence. He promised to come back the next weekend and put up a loafing shed for some hay and shelter against the elements, and he did. I think the men worked for beer, but I don't know about the money for the pasture, where Mom came up with it. Those things never occurred to me then. I just wanted life to work, and when it did I didn't ask questions.

On the pavement outside the trailer, Gram and I had bathed Gabe with her Breck so that his coat looked almost as silvery and lustrous as usual. Gram put iodine on the cuts, and I put Vaseline on the outside of his hooves — a useless gesture for a horse in pasture, but I wanted him to feel my care as I held each hoof in my hand and massaged the petroleum into it.

For a water trough, we scrubbed out an empty garbage can and filled it with a garden hose we ran across the pavement and into the pasture. I was happy when at last he was in the pasture and he ambled up to the can, drinking long and deep from it. I stood by the bay window and watched him until dusk bled out into night.

OF ALL THE YEARS WE SPENT TOGETHER, Gabe and I, the images of that day play back as if they were happening now. Maybe it's because the day signaled the first in a series of times I would not be able to protect he who had protected me.

Eventually I was lucky enough to get out of the trailer park, first as an exchange student and then to college. Gabe, well over twenty years old by then, was turned out to pasture on a nearby horse farm, acres of lush grass. An idyllic retirement.

After a while, though, money got tight — again — and we fell behind in the board for his care. I didn't find this out until one Easter when I went back to the Enchanted Hills, Lot no. 78, on a break from school. I was ferreting around in the shed, looking for Gabe's halter, when my Gram asked me what the hell I was doing out there.

"I thought I'd go over to that farm and see if I can't catch the old guy in the pasture. Maybe take him out bareback," I told her.

And then I saw the look on her face, the pinched corners around her mouth. "What?" I said. "What?"

"Oh, Sammy," and I knew by her calling me by my childhood name that she meant to deliver bad news.

The story she told was that she had sold Gabe to a children's summer camp to pay off the back board. I asked her the name of the place; she said she'd have to look up the papers, and the papers were buried away in the cedar chest. And I shed a few tears at that, but then imagined happy children's faces as they sat on what was now his swayback and bounced at his choppy trot. I imagined his big hay belly growing fatter, his mane ever shaggier.

But then a few days later I woke up in the middle of the night, my heart pounding, my chest so tight I couldn't gulp enough air. There were no children's camps around here. And even if they'd shipped him somewhere else, what kind of a camp would take an ancient, swaybacked gelding? Gram, a horsewoman, would know only one kind of horse buyer would be interested in such a prospect, and that was the feed-lot buyer, headed for the slaughterhouses in Texas.

No.

Nonononono.

Then, another possibility occurred to me. Maybe Gabe had merely died, as old horses will, and Gram, not wanting to upset me, made up a story — truth never having much currency in our home as it was.

The only way to know for sure would be to go to the farm and ask. Once Gram committed to a story, she was not one to change it. So, I made a plan to go there the next morning.

Except, I didn't.

Either way, I knew how powerless I was. I was a college student lucky to make my tuition every semester. Of the three possible fates for my Gabriel, one offered me comfort, another sadness but acceptance, and the final one more anguish than I could possibly deal with. And so I took the path of not knowing, which, as the years have gone by, has meant a kind of purgatory, the image of a white horse forever invoking my lost Gabriel, angel of mercy.

IN MOLLY'S EYES

Billy Mernit

We know the ones we love by the things they love.

Molly loved to dig. Left on her own, she'd transform any likely patch of ground into a whorl of flying dirt.

She loved the car. If we were taking a road trip, she'd go sit inside it long before we were due to leave. I'd find Molly behind the wheel, upright and eager in the driver's seat, as if impatient to peel out with me as her passenger.

She loved to destroy things left within her reach and was endowed with a cast-iron stomach. She chewed, and eschewed nothing: shoes, pens, even double-A batteries became fodder and then debris.

She loved to burrow to the bottom of a sleeping bag or bed. Though she slept tucked beneath a blanket in her living room chair (good thing, since her snoring was robust), she'd trot in during the early morning hours to paw at my bedside till I sleepily pulled aside the covers so she could crawl into the depths.

She loved Thomas the cairn terrier, a quarter of her size and power and endowed with an ear-bruising bark. Molly's maternal side surfaced when she wrestled with him, an endless entertainment. They'd leap and roll and fall upon each other like a pair of mismatched movie dinosaurs, teeth ferociously bared, but Molly moderated the intensity of her attacks so that Thomas never got injured. She'd endure his lunges and nips like an old boxing coach indulging a newbie-in-training.

She loved to run. She'd been hell in her wild youth. There was a long, deep scar around her neck, from the time she dashed out of a dog park to be hit by a car.

A scar on her right side was the ghost of a cancer. Maybe these brushes with death contributed to Molly's mature equanimity. By the time I met her, she wasn't easily excitable. She was calm in repose, and her long nose gave her face a sleek femininity instead of the squat, bullish look of your average Am-Staff. Like Petey from *Our Gang*, she had one eye encircled by a patch of brown fur on her white face, and that eye was haloed in black, as if mascaraed. Possessing a soulful gaze with a centuries-old stare, Molly had a regal air of autonomy. When she chose to sit beside you, you felt privileged.

QUALIFIED LOVE: WE HAVE PLENTY OF THAT — from ex-lovers, step-siblings, de-frienders. Live long enough, and the chambers of your heart will be lined with the shrouds of expired passions. The love that never questions, that never swerves from its devotion, seems more common to the movies. Too many of us hear of it only in pop songs.

I count myself among the lucky few who have walked down that paradisiacal path. So I'm not here to complain about what's gone, because love of the purest strain lives on. It's as strong and everlasting as the loss.

CERTAIN PEOPLE ARE PORTALS. You meet them and your world widens, deepens. My wife-to-be, Judith, came with two dogs and two cats. I walked with her into the animal world. The felines were an easy add-on, and Thomas, a dead ringer for Toto, was suffused with cute-osity. But when I first met Molly on the end of Judith's leash, she terrified me. Knowing nothing of the truth, I thought all pit bulls were enraged and homicidal. In that first view of Molly, an introduction as cue-thunder ominous as a horror movie clip, she was a shadowy, bulky figure who seemed bigger than Judith. All that was missing was the chewed-off human hand clomped between her massive jaws.

Yet as I fell in love with the owner, I began to get comfortable with the dog. Judith and I were by then living side by side in adjacent units of a bungalow in Venice Beach. On nights when I came home before Judith and puttered around my apartment, I assumed that the barking next door was the dogs' standard response to hearing a human nearby. When I walked over to let them out, Molly bounded up to me with intense excitement, doing a crazed butt-wiggling dance of celebration, whining with happiness, batting her long head against my thighs. I figured she was doing what any dog did when released from human-less confinement, but Judith chastised me for keeping Molly waiting and making her so unhappy. "She's barking because she wants to be with *you*," she explained.

Suddenly I had a dog. Every morning, Molly would ask to be let out of Judith's place. Judith would let her out. Molly would then walk around the back of the bungalow and come knocking on my door. Once admitted, she'd trot right up into an armchair she'd claimed as hers on one of her first visits. From there, she surveyed the domain or stared at me adoringly.

I was her dutiful bitch in no time.

A Few Things that Bonding with a Dog Introduces You To:

The local trees and greenery — sidewalks, and the lawns.

The number of objects that might be edible.

The pleasures of sitting in the sun, among them the ability to suspend time.

Every other dog in existence. As well as the world of foolhardy squirrels.

MOLLY HAD RAISED JUDITH'S CATS — two orphaned brother-and-sister kittens — from birth, saving their tiny lives with her faux-mom ministrations, so why should it have been surprising that she would adopt me? She used to hold down the Bean and then his sister, Flower, while she thoroughly licked their nether regions clean, the cats yowling protests, Molly impervious, so I could imagine her thought process in sizing me up: Thinks he doesn't need a dog, does he? I'll set 'em straight.

Having never experienced dog devotion, I was flummoxed when this gentle, kindhearted babe of an animal made her claim on me. Molly was all about the tribe — on the trail, she'd be lead dog, but she'd periodically run back to make sure you were coming along, and if you got up from a city gathering to go to the bathroom, she'd shepherd you both ways — but this was different. If Judith and I were walking Thomas and Molly, and I had to leave the group for any reason, she'd use her hind legs like superbrakes, refusing to walk onward.

By now the very notion of Molly wanting to harm any living thing seemed far-fetched, about as likely as her taking up the saxophone. But one time I did see her become genuinely vicious for an instant. A drunk whose tats and attitude suggested some acquaintance with gang life stopped by our restaurant patio table to admire Molly. Quiet and stoic as usual, she endured his pets and praises until he lurched too close to me to make a point. With an ugly growl, she leapt at him — just close enough to scare the lights out of us both and to let me know that she would, in fact, rip someone's throat to protect her man.

Why was it, how was it, that this muscle-headed beast looked to me first, followed me from room to room, and whimpered until I returned to the herd? The dog heart wants what it wants, but what was it in me that Molly wanted?

Possible Qualities That Might Make Me Lovable to a Dog:

I've noticed that humans are often subliminally drawn to mates who resemble them in some way. The union of one couple I know announces: we're in love with this nose. Was Molly of the aquiline snout attracted to mine?

It couldn't have been my sense of humor, or my being so well read. The famous people I knew? Irrelevant. She wasn't into me for my convertible alone, cool as it was.

The cynic in me thought: adaptive behavior — I was simply a secondary provider (next to Judith, I was a push-over in terms of treat indulgence) and thus required extra attention. Thing was, Molly had literally and figuratively gone over to my side, so there had to be some intuitive attraction to the me-ness of me operative here. She might've liked my smell. Judith argues that I have a calmer nature than hers, and so Molly took to me in relief. This kind of love is like an eye of God, though. I felt that what she cleaved to was the best of me, even if I didn't quite know what that was.

I did know how to stroke her, in a certain way, on the very softest hair of her brow. This was my method of love transmission, which I know she welcomed. One night as I sat talking to Judith, I was stroking Molly's chest with one hand. When I stopped the absent petting and started to rise, she put her paw on my chest, forbidding my exit. The message was clear as she gazed into my eyes: Don't stop.

For days afterward, "She's giving me the paw!" was my delighted cry. After a while, this became routine: whenever I petted or stroked her, her paw demanded more.

IT STARTED ON A CAMPING TRIP, with a cough from Molly late one night so loud it woke the couple in a neighboring tent. The cough took, and it led to increasingly prolonged fits. I brought her to our vet, thinking we'd get her medicine or a minor procedure. I was summoned to an office with surprising urgency, where the doctor stood contemplating an X-ray as though she were the first on the scene of a car wreck. An insidiously clever tumor had wrapped itself around one of Molly's lungs and her aorta, classically inoperable. Really, what we were looking at was a matter of time.

Molly prided herself in her vigilant alertness, so she hated the canine Vicodin that suppressed her cough. Even when the medicine was embedded in her favorite foods, she'd outsmart us, getting the food down and spitting out the pill. The drugs gave her respite, but she'd fight the effects. Refusing to lie down, she'd sit up beside the couch and slowly, slowly, tilt, like a junkie on the nod, until she hung at a forty-five-degree angle over the floor. Then she'd finally let me guide her into a supine position.

One day Molly was out in the garden and, in a reprise of her old enthusiasm, began to dig furiously by the steps. After a moment of it, her cough kicked in and she stopped, gazing up at me with a mixture of bewilderment and pain that ripped right at my heart. "Why is this happening?" she was asking, and worse, "Why can't you make it stop?" I led her back inside and stroked the soft fur on her chest until she quieted down.

Judith was out of town one night when Molly got caught in a fit that would not quit. She was gasping for breath. I alerted the hospital, which was twenty minutes away even with no traffic, and drove at demon speed, Molly wheezing in the back seat while I prayed to no God I'd ever paged before. When we got there, she was too weak to climb from the car, so I carried her to the elevator, stumbling, horrified to see her pee on the floor — a shocking breach of dignity that upped my alarm. As soon as the doors opened upstairs, I was yelling like a character in a bad TV movie, "This dog needs oxygen!"

The interns hurried over to take her from me. I paced for a few awful minutes until one emerged to tell me she was tented and breathing normally. It had been no false alarm: another few minutes, and Molly would've been gone.

I'D BEEN UNUSUALLY FORTUNATE for many years: since losing my grandparents decades earlier, death hadn't come this close.

We had planned a weekend trip to the mountains for Molly to enjoy. But it was bitter cold, the town was inordinately busy with tourists, and Molly's now-constant wheezing was frightening small children. "What's wrong with that dog?" a little girl asked her concerned mother as they passed us on the street. When we got back to the cabin we'd rented for the weekend, Molly lay on the bed with a baleful look on her face that was unmistakable. Judith had been saying for some time now that Molly would let us know. We made the necessary call and cut the trip short.

Back home, we invited Molly to lie in bed alongside us. I wrapped myself around her warm girth and nuzzled her like a fellow dog. We try to inhale the ones who are leaving. We're holding on to what's been revealed to be a transitory thing. Molly was by then deeply involved with the simple task of continuing to breathe, and her gaze had dulled. She no longer brightened when I sat down beside her.

Judith grilled her a steak for her last dinner. Molly ate it with care and concentration. The next morning, when the doctor came, we took her for a last short walk, and she made a rare show of animation. It was as if she sensed what the stranger's visit signified. She, too, was postponing the inevitable. She seemed to be greeting and saying good-bye to the sun, grass, and wind.

The doctor explained a series of injections. We stroked her as the first needle went in, kissed her brow as the sedative seeped through her bloodstream. This was the prep for the second injection's lethal chemical, but Molly had stopped breathing, her eyes closed. The doctor was surprised to confirm that she was already gone. Her heart had been doing hard, hard work. It must've been such relief to at last let go.

Judith and I cried then, supporting each other like a suddenly elderly couple. There was an emptiness in the house that had never been there before. We hurried to put away the things of hers that now were merely things.

AND LESS THAN A YEAR LATER, when I had to cope with my father's passing, I realized there was something familiar in it, that I was deeper into the heart of a dark country whose territory was not entirely unknown. If a person who's trying to process a beloved parent's demise is so much raw human meat, you could say that I'd already been tenderized. Molly did this for me. She left me this brute knowledge as a kind of parting gift.

Her bones and ashes sit in a wooden box atop the bookshelves by my bed, but this is only totem and fetish, a shaker flung by a shaman toward the relentless infinity of sky. The bones aren't Molly, just as what's in the box that arrived for my mother, some days after his cremation, is decidedly not my dad. Where we go is the one thing that we can't know, but I like to think spirit moves on. A new kind of conversation evokes it in each newly precious day. And memory...

THE SHRUB SHAKES, as if there's an isolated earthquake in our garden. Little clods of earth shoot out from behind it, and I can see a blur of light brown fur beyond the green. Molly's digging. I step out onto the front stoop to get a better look. She's gotten down to the depths of this hole, her white chest hair flecked with the darker dirt, paws a rhythmic blur. She backs up to assess her work, panting, circles the hole amidst the weeds, and then settles herself into it with unmistakable satisfaction, hind legs tucked beneath her, front legs crossed. Body in the shade, head in the sun, she turns her face to me, teeth glinting, tongue dripping, dark eyes serene. She smiles at me, and rests her chin on her paws. Guarding the gates to heaven.

12

WINESBURG

Barbara Abercrombie

The sign said, "Kittens for sale," and I thought, why not? I'd just had lunch with my Aunt Helen, complete with cocktails, so I was feeling awfully good and not overly practical as I swayed into the dingy pet shop — though the word *practical* wasn't really in my vocabulary. I was nineteen years old, had just dropped out of college to become an actress in New York, had very little money, and lived in a railroad apartment that had a front window held together by duct tape.

I picked up one of the kittens — flea-bitten, ribs showing, coal black, and much too young to have been taken from its mother. It needed to be rescued. After two daiquiris on a hot September afternoon this seemed like a terrific idea. Why not? I paid the five dollars, took the kitten home, gave her a bath to get rid of the fleas, and came up with a name for her.

"*Winesburg*?" said one of my roommates as the kitten climbed our curtains.

"As in Ohio," I said. My current boyfriend was in a Broadway play based on Sherwood Anderson's book *Winesburg, Ohio*.

Besides curtain climbing, Winesburg loved to hide under the beds, then reach out for passing ankles and hang on with her claws. (I ended up buying my roommates a lot of new stockings.) Winesburg's favorite trick was to grab the end of the roll of toilet paper between her teeth and then race from the bathroom through the rooms of the long narrow apartment, unfurling toilet paper like a banner behind her.

"I don't find this cat TP-ing the apartment very funny," said one of my roommates as she unwrapped the chairs and couch.

Granted, Winesburg was not a cozy, cuddly little kitten, and yes, she was kind of crazy and wild, but we were a good fit.

We traveled a lot — on the train up to Westchester to visit my family on weekends, and then, when I got acting jobs on Broadway, to Philadelphia and Washington, D.C., for out-of-town tryouts. Winesburg loved the excitement of escaping from hotel rooms, and then, hissing and spitting, she'd hold armies of housekeepers and bellmen at bay as they tried to capture her. When I played the ingénue in a cross-country tour of *Pleasure of His Company*, starring Joan Bennett, Winesburg attacked Miss Bennett's poodle, Tinker Bell, and my parents had to come take my cat back to Westchester for the remainder of the tour. "It's not like she's an *easy* cat," said my mother as Winesburg's cat carrier was loaded into their car.

After the tour I found an apartment I could afford on my own, and while it was being painted, Winesburg and I camped out at my friend Nicki's place on the fourteenth floor at Park Avenue and Eighty-sixth Street — much more posh surroundings than we were used to. Late one night I couldn't find Winesburg. "How the hell can a cat disappear from the fourteenth floor?" I cried.

Nicki and I looked at each other, suddenly horrified. We knew exactly how — the windows had no screens and there was only a ten-inch ledge under them. We raced down to the street. The doorman assured us that no cats had fallen out of the building that evening. I calmed down and thought about how Winesburg was Houdini. She was a master of hiding in strange and unlikely places — and it was a big apartment. That's what had happened; I figured she'd come out when she was ready.

At dawn the next morning the doorbell rang. It was the couple across the hall. The woman was holding Winesburg. She apologized for waking us so early and asked if this was our cat.

"Yes, yes," I said, grabbing my beloved. "Where was she?"

"She came through our window last night and got into bed with us," said the man. "Let me tell you, it was quite a shock."

That ledge was only ten inches wide. How brave she was!

WHEN I MARRIED MY FIRST HUSBAND, a lieutenant in the navy, I followed him to Vietnam on a tourist visa, and of course Winesburg came too.

"You brought the *cat* with you?" said my new husband, looking aghast when Winesburg's crate arrived with me at Tan Son Nhat International Airport. "*Winesburg* came too?"

"I wrote you about finding kitty litter in Saigon —"

"I thought it was a *joke*."

"My beloved cat is not a joke," I said, briefly wondering why I had married this man.

The three of us checked into the Continental Palace Hotel in Saigon, Winesburg none the worse for her twelve-thousand-mile trip. A week later we moved into a rented house at 64B Hung Tap Tu across the street from the French embassy. It was impossible to keep Winesburg inside, and she roamed the neighborhood — down the street to the Buddhist school and over to the embassy. "La chat noir est à la recherche d'un amant!" the guard would say when I'd come looking for my cat, the black cat who was looking for love.

Winesburg and I lived in Saigon for almost a year, until the war escalated and dependants had to be evacuated. Though I had come over on a tourist visa and paid my own way, I qualified as a dependant, and one morning a very young officer, his uniform crisp as toast, was sent to the house on Hung Tap Tu to notify me of the evacuation plans. Apparently it was a very big deal — the generals' and admirals' wives were being evacuated, and General Westmoreland would be at Tan Son Nhat International Airport in person to say good-bye.

"What about my cat?" I asked.

"Your cat, ma'am?"

"I have a cat. She has to be evacuated too."

"Ma'am, we have no arrangements for cats to be evacuated from Vietnam."

"Then I can't possibly leave."

He struggled for composure. "You must leave." He had dropped the brisk military tone and was pleading. "This is an evacuation. You can't stay. It's a *war*."

"Then somebody's got to resolve my cat issue."

"The navy will look into it," he said and fled.

We'd be going home via Hawaii — which posed another problem. Even if I could get Winesburg on the evacuation flight, she wouldn't be able to land and change planes with me in Honolulu because of the animal quarantine restrictions that were then in effect. Eventually, at my expense, arrangements were made to evacuate Winesburg home to New York in the other direction — on Air France via Paris.

WINESBURG SURVIVED VIETNAM and the evacuation and went on to live in all the apartments and houses of my first marriage. She sat on every table and desk I wrote on, slept in every bed, was jealous when my babies were born, and suffered the addition of other cats and Newfoundlands to the family with initial outrage and claw swipes. But she was always First Cat. The cat with the longest history, the most personality, the hottest temper, and also the most beautiful. By the time we moved into her last house, she had mellowed. She was deaf by then, and every morning she would slowly make her way to the pool to sit gazing at reflections in the water. Watching her, I'd think what a long journey we'd had from our New York apartments and the house on Hung Tap Tu to Palos Verdes, California.

Winesburg died on September 26, 1977, at 4:30 in the afternoon. She was nineteen years old. Her kidneys were failing, and she couldn't stand or drink water. I prayed that she'd die at home, but she began to suffer, and late in the afternoon I rushed her to the vet. He said her heart was going. He shaved a patch of fur on her front leg. I held her and he slipped the needle in. And she was gone.

I didn't know how hard it would be after. How final and silent. How gone she would be. I felt as if a family member had died — but this was a family member who had known me much longer than my husband and children had known me. The link to my past was gone. I felt as if she took those years with her. Half my life in fact.

I went to bed and cried for three days. I saw her everywhere — in shadows, in dark sweaters tossed at random, in glimpses of our other animals. Finally I got up and went on with my life, but I continued to mourn her for a long time, feeling very much alone and even embarrassed at the depth of my grief. This was before support groups were thought of for dealing with the deaths of pets, before sympathy cards that acknowledged the loss of an animal, a time when well-meaning friends suggested that I get another black cat right away.

As I write about her today, I dig out old journals to find her stories. I email my ex-husband, who apparently has managed to wipe his memory clear of Winesburg. I call my friend Nicki, who had the apartment on the fourteenth floor, and she says, "That was the meanest cat I ever met, sneaky too. She ruined all my stockings. She was crazy." Then I email my brother, who writes back, "She was vicious! Remember, once she even scratched Mom? She only liked you."

I have absolutely no memory of Winesburg ever attacking my mother. She certainly wasn't a vicious cat; she was high-spirited. Perhaps not an easy cat, not cuddly and cozy, but memorable and beloved. And oh, how fiercely I loved her. Even after all these years I can still feel that love in my heart. But here's the thing about losing an animal that I have had to learn over and over again — when I let myself grieve I come to the end of it. And finally the tears open my heart to the animals who follow.

13.

PARTY GIRL

Monica Holloway

My husband, Michael, and I had been married only three months when we began frequenting the local animal shelters. It took two weekends to find her, and I'm surprised it took that long. The holdup was: "Do we get a short-haired or a long-haired dog?" In the end, that turned out to be as superficial as it sounded. When we saw our girl, we knew.

We'd been to shelters in Pasadena, Glendale, and Santa Monica all in one morning and had almost given up; in fact, Michael was heading to the parking lot when I made my final loop through the West Los Angeles Animal Shelter. Peering into the kennels, I leaned over and looked under one of the steel benches. There she was, lying on her back, legs splayed to the side and her ears flopped back against the cement floor, their pink interior soft and kissable. Her fur was long and black with a body-wave fluffiness that rivaled anything

L'Oréal could have produced. There was a birthmark on her tummy shaped exactly like Texas.

When I pointed to her, the volunteer tried to wake her, but she stretched her paws into the air, sighing into an even deeper sleep. So, putting his hands on either side of her body, he carefully slid her over to the metal mesh door. I leaned down and put my palm on Texas. Her head was still thrown back so that her teeth were showing. She had a darling overbite, just like my new groom's.

"Shepherd mix," the volunteer told me. "Probably shepherd-collie."

She was mostly black, but now I could see that in the center of her chest was white fur — as if she'd been dyed black and a dessert plate, perfectly round, had covered that particular spot. When she finally sat up, her ears looked like fuzzy tortilla chips with the top of the triangle folded down, and she had a narrow, pointed collie snout. Her eyelashes were elegant and long, giving her a look of sophistication beyond her years — or lack of years. The shelter estimated that she was only about three months old.

When I picked her up, the volunteer said, "That's gonna be a big dog. Look at those paws."

"Don't tell my husband," I pleaded, holding the puppy up to my nose and sniffing in her essence.

Michael and I had agreed on a small-to-medium dog because we lived in an apartment, but that treaty was about to change.

I carried the puppy to the front window and motioned for Michael, who had pulled the car around and was waiting for me to get in so we could move on to the next shelter. I held her up for him to see. Pointing to the top of her head, I mouthed, "Yes! Yes! Yes?"

He laughed, turned the car off, and grabbed our checkbook out of the glove compartment.

Forty-five dollars to adopt and spay her.

She was ours. We named her Hallie.

IT'S MARCH NOW, and sixteen years later you can probably still make out Texas, but Hallie doesn't like to be on her back anymore. After all, she's "one hundred and twelve years old in human years," as our son, Wills, likes to point out. So I haven't seen Texas in a long time.

Her muzzle is still dark, with gray showing only under her chin, blending into the white-dessert-plate patch of fur on her chest. She's not oil-black anymore, but rather slate — her curls still swirling around her torso. Her eyes are cloudy, but alert. She can no longer hear.

We're saying our good-byes every day. Hallie has an inoperable brain tumor on the right side of her head. "Six months," the vet told us more than eight months ago, and when, before Christmas, she began to fail, it looked like he just might be right. She wandered around in a confused state, not recognizing any of us — Wills, whom she'd practically delivered herself when I was thrown into labor early one May morning, or Michael or me. She was urinating on the carpets and hardwood floors without even realizing it.

But New Year's Eve 2009 came, and when she made it past midnight, I guessed that this meant something to her — something more significant than the people around her tossing wishes into the fire pit outside and watching the wind carry the embers to God or the universe or wherever wishes and prayers and hopes go. To Hallie, she'd made it one more year, and here was another one staring her down. She wouldn't waste time on wishing; she'd need to live — right then. She started on New Year's Day.

I woke to find her standing by our bed staring at me, her chin resting on the white down comforter. She hadn't done that in over five years. She was hungry. I rubbed the soft fur between her ears. She hobbled to the door and looked back as if to say, "You're supposed to follow me." This was another "Hallie-ism" we hadn't seen in a very long time. I jumped up and followed her to the kitchen with Michael right behind me.

"Hallie's back," I told Michael, watching the can of Wellness food twirling around on the can opener. The whirring sound alerted our two golden retrievers, and soon there were three dogs wiggling with anticipation right by the back door. I carried out their plates.

Leo Henry, our new puppy, was barely five months, and Buddy Rose was three years old. We'd gotten Buddy shortly after the death of our beloved golden retriever, Cowboy. She'd been a source of great healing for all of us, but especially my son, who had high-functioning autism and needed stability and, more important, a puppy in his life. We'd discovered this by accident shortly after Cowboy had arrived and Wills began to improve in ways we hadn't thought possible.

Hallie wasn't a child's dog, although she was fiercely protective of Wills. She preferred adults, who were more practical and less likely to surprise her. Generally, she liked to stay in the background and watch and listen. She had no interest in romping or playing. Cowboy, however, was game for anything silly, muddy, or childlike. She was Wills's companion, but Hallie was Big Sister, making sure that no one came through our front gate or hurt him in any way.

On New Year's morning, Hallie watched the Rose Bowl Parade with us, sitting on the carpet with Buddy and Leo Henry. She wasn't wandering around the house, anxious and crying for no reason as she had during the last couple of years. When it came time to potty, she pulled herself up and made it to the backyard without assistance.

"Look at our Hallie," I told Wills.

"It's like she's taken 'Happy New Year' to a whole new level," Michael said.

"She's happy," Wills chimed in.

"She really *does* look happy," I smiled. Hallie had been spending most of her days sleeping on a fluffy striped comforter that we'd draped over her round dog bed in our front room. It was good to have her awake and right in the middle of things.

I remembered something our friend Lynn had said the night before at our New Year's Eve party. Watching Hallie weaving in and out of people's legs, she observed, "You know, Hallie might not want to be petted or loved on, but she sure wants to be at the party."

THIRTEEN YEARS AGO, when Hallie was our only dog, she was still very much at the party, a wallflower to be sure, but always within sight. She loved being home, and saw the world mostly through the car window, preferring long rides sitting on my lap as I drove, her paws poised on my window-sill, eyes squinting into the wind.

When I became pregnant with Wills, I was so nauseous that I spent every morning and evening lying on the cool bathroom tiles close to the toilet. Hallie always lay down beside me, carefully placing her soft, black chin against my cheek. It was stifling hot, but she could sense that I needed her, and that's what she could give. We laid there, sometimes for hours, the side of my face sweaty and draped in fur.

When baby Wills finally came home from the hospital, Hallie was very confused by the new person in her pack. But once she realized he was here to stay, she went on high alert. Her job, she'd decided, was to protect both baby and mother.

While I sat in the white rocker nursing Wills, Hallie would sit on my feet facing out, keeping watch in all directions. No offer of food or rubber balls could budge her from her post. Same as the pregnancy, the nursing made me so hot, and with her heavy coat of hair draped on my feet, I felt like I might spontaneously combust. But it was such a tender gesture and a great comfort to have her there that I didn't have the heart to ask her to move.

Hallie was suspicious of all deliveries, including the daily visits from our poor mailman, Tony. When he entered our yard, she'd go wild, barking and racing back and forth in the front hallway. Tony would drop the mail through the slot in the front door and race back to the safety of the sidewalk. He was an ex-marine, but he'd also had the unfortunate experience of meeting Hallie in the yard one day when he'd stopped to say hello to Wills, who was sitting on a blanket next to me. Hallie was furious that this person was so close to Wills, so she chased Tony across the grass, barking and nipping at the backs of his ankles. I was mortified, but also knew that no one would be robbing our house. No one could even get near it. Michael installed a mailbox outside our picket fence just for Tony.

Any type of truck made Hallie crazy, and she raised hell whenever one drove by. One cloudy afternoon, she took on the UPS truck. As Spencer, our favorite UPS driver, rounded the corner, Hallie jumped our front picket fence and raced toward the truck. Luckily, Spencer stopped in time, albeit barely. I could smell the burnt tires from him stomping on the brakes to avoid hitting her. She sat inches from the grille, looking over at me with a satisfied look on her face. We built a higher fence.

Hallie loved to be higher than anyone else. She ran our canyon hiking trails nimbly and fast, dashing to the top of rolling hills and then kicking up the light brown dirt on her way back down, beige powder forming a cloud around her delicate legs.

Wills was about four years old when we were hiking at Tree People Park. He'd gone several steps ahead of me and Hallie was right beside him. Suddenly, Hallie began to bark. Wills ran back and said, "A spider is walking."

"What color?" I asked him.

"Brown. Hallie is mad at it," he replied, pointing down the path.

Hallie was standing stock-still, her nose to the ground. I pictured a small brown wolf spider or something equally benign, but when I got to where she was, her nose was resting on top of a tarantula. She wasn't moving, and neither was the spider. She was waiting for Wills and me to go by. We did, quickly, and then I called her. She did a little hop step back and came running. The spider scrambled down a hole and a small chipmunk came running out as if he'd been shot out of a cannon.

"Boy, that was close," I said, my mouth dry from fear.

"A tarantula will bite, Mommy, but it's not serious," Wills said, running slightly ahead. I caught up with him.

"Really?" I asked. "I thought they were poisonous."

"I don't want to get bitten," he said, "by anything."

"Me, neither," I agreed.

"So it's good that Hallie did that," he said. "Tarantulas go bald on their thorax when they get old." He picked up a stick for Hallie. Wills's autism contributed to his almost photographic memory. We had read about tarantulas two years earlier, and yet he knew every fact we'd uncovered.

"It *is* good that she did that," I told him. "Imagine how big that spider must have looked to her."

Maybe the spider hadn't intimidated her, because Hallie had seen it all in her eight years. The menagerie of animals that had come through our house since Wills turned three included hamsters, hermit crabs, dumpy frogs, land turtles, rabbits, and, of course, the retrievers. Hallie watched them come and go with stoic bemusement, curious, but not really bothered by any of it.

She shielded us, that was her job — especially when it came to Wills. There was deep love between them, but it was as if Hallie were a protective aunt, standoffish but fiercely protective. And in January, two weeks after our New Year's Eve party, Wills returned the favor.

WILLS WAS TWELVE YEARS OLD when, on a sunny Saturday afternoon, he, Buddy, Leo Henry, and Hallie were walking toward the shallow end of our pool. I was on the patio, closer to the house but watching them go. As they started around the deep end, Leo Henry saw a tennis ball floating in the water and dove for it. When he plunged into the water, he accidentally knocked Hallie into the pool. Hallie had always been an excellent swimmer, but hadn't been in water for over six years. She sank like a stone. Her back legs were not agile enough to push her to the top and her front paws were equally unreliable.

I ran toward the pool, but I didn't need to. Wills, my boy who was anything but spontaneous, who usually refused to swim unless he was wearing goggles that covered his nose *and* eyes, and who was fastidious about not getting his clothes wet, instantaneously leaped into the water wearing sweatpants, a hooded sweatshirt, and a pair of fleece-lined Ugg boots. He even had on his beloved Mets cap, a gift given to him by his late grandfather and something that he cherished. By the time they'd made it to the side of the pool, Hallie's head was above water and Wills was underneath, holding her up and paddling his feet. He swam them both to the shallow end.

Wills's Mets cap was now lying at the bottom of the deep end. I hurried to meet them at the steps.

"Wills, oh my gosh, I can't believe Leo knocked her in," I said, "and she went right under."

"She can't swim," he sputtered, water coming out of his nose and mouth.

"You saved her life," I told him, lifting first Hallie and then Wills out of the pool. "You saved Hallie's life." I wiped his face with the bottom of my T-shirt and cradled a wet and shaky Hallie in my arms.

"It's lucky I was here," he said, suddenly smiling.

"Yes, it was," I said, slipping one of my arms around his waist.

"I weigh about fifty pounds more than when I was dry," he said, standing up. As he headed toward the house, his Uggs squished pools of water onto the tiles.

"Hallie was always a great swimmer, but now we know she can't hold herself up," I said, my voice almost a whisper as I imagined both of them at the bottom of the pool struggling. After all, Wills loved to be in the pool, but he wasn't the best swimmer. But that's not what happened — at all. "Let's get you inside," I said, lifting Hallie. Meanwhile, Leo Henry and Buddy began their nightly doggy laps in the pool.

After wrapping Hallie in a beach towel, I put Wills right into a hot shower, his pajamas lying on the bathroom counter. Hallie was so thin with her wavy hair stuck to her body, I happily held her on my lap and waited for Wills.

That night, I asked Wills if I could call some of our friends and tell them that he was a hero. "Yes," he said, "I think that you should." He smiled and leaned against me on the couch listening as I told the story over and over again.

IT'S NOW JULY and we've been in this strange time with Hallie for a while now, where we know there might not be much time left, have been told as much. She's begun peeing and pooping on the carpet again and seems disoriented, even with the medication we've been giving her. Still, she has her good days.

The family room carpet needs to be replaced. Between Hallie's bathroom problems and Leo Henry's difficulty potty training, it's like living inside a litter box. But we're reluctant to go to the carpet store. So I have to ask myself, "What are we waiting for?" — even though I know the answer. No one wants to say it, but we're waiting for the unthinkable. We're waiting for Hallie to go.

"Wouldn't it be a shame to get new carpet only to have her pee on it?" my friend Emily asked. Yes, it would. But that ruined carpet reminds me every day that I'm literally waiting for Hallie to die. I can't do that to her or myself. Hallie's getting on with living, and so will we. Michael and I ordered new carpet — and long plastic runners to cover it.

We're going to quit saying good-bye before she's even gone.

THIS MORNING, Wills's very last hamster, Teddy, died. He was four years old — our longest-living hamster (and we've had at least twelve of them through the years). I found him on his side, his head resting on the bottom of his red wire wheel and his front paws relaxed and casual against his tiny chest. Teddy's eyes weren't open but his mouth was, revealing he was so old that he'd lost one of his elongated front teeth.

I picked him up in a blue washcloth — his body still soft. Hallie was standing beside me, so I knelt down and let her sniff him. She gave him a good once over and then looked at me as if to say, "Damn, your animals have lousy constitutions."

"You'll outlive us all," I told her, kissing the top of her head. She followed me to the bedroom, where I picked out the perfect shoebox. It had to be plain, because Wills decorated all shoeboxes used for burying pets with plastic jewels, colored leaves, and special writings about what made that animal unique.

I laid Teddy in the box, wrapping the washcloth loosely around him so just his tiny face was showing. I placed the shoebox on the fireplace mantle to wait for Wills.

Sitting on the hearth, I took Hallie's face in my hands.

Buddy and Leo were hiking with Michael and Wills, so it was just Hallie and me. Her back legs were sticking out to the sides in an awkward slant. I couldn't help but wish she'd give up on those back legs for a little while and just sit or lie down. Standing looked so painful. But Hallie never gave up.

I looked into her eyes, but it didn't seem as if my image was getting past the cataracts. Still, she held her snout up for me to kiss. She'd lived with us at our first apartment in West Hollywood, at our house on Beverly Glen Boulevard, at the crazy house on Camarillo Street, and now here, in the home we finally owned.

I don't know where the years went; I don't know how long it's been since she was capable of jumping up onto our bed with one gentle leap, or how long since she could hear well enough to howl at a fire truck whizzing by us. Too long. Still, she's here, and that's what matters. She might be wobbly, but she's not in pain. The brain tumor is benign, but getting bigger. We have no idea what direction that will take in the next few months.

My heart's been broken with many losses through the years, but there have been enormous blessings, too. Wills was born; my career has evolved; my son has grown into an adorable, smart, funny adolescent; my roots turned gray along with Hallie's; I survived a heart attack. Old friends came and went and then came back again. My marriage broke apart for more than a year, and I cried until my chest nearly collapsed. I painted the house and bought a new grill. My husband came back.

Hallie, this girl who's always preferred to stay in the background, choosing when she wants kisses or hugs, has been the one constant through the years, completely devoted but asking for nothing in return.

I carefully load her into the car, plastic underneath her blanket just in case she has to pee. I lift her up, mindful not to hurt her fragile bones and joints as I place her on the passenger seat. She can no longer sit on my lap and hang her head out the window. It's too exhausting for her to hold herself up.

Tonight we'll bury the hamster, but this afternoon Hallie and I are going for a ride.

14.

A RELIGION NAMED YOYO

Linzi Glass

School assembly. Rows of hot, cheese-smelling socks lined up on the polished floor. No black-soled shoes were allowed to scuff up the ancient wood in the auditorium, according to our principal, Mr. Coldry. Outside, hundreds of pairs waited in neat rows to be claimed after we had been dismissed. Just thinking about the task of finding my shoes, the ones with one lace shorter than the other, made my hands clammy.

Inside, mouths moved, voices were raised in song. Backs were straight and eyes lifted to the teachers on the podium. Lips were parted in perfect O's. Everyone's but mine — they were clamped shut. My tongue trapped behind rigid teeth as the others sang, "Jesus loves me this I know, for the Bible tells me so." Voices blending one into the other, louder now, eyes bright with joy. Jesus, yes, Jesus was their savior. Everyone's but mine. I was small and dark haired, a replica of my grandmother, Leah, so I had been told, although I had never met her. She had died giving birth to my mother, Ruth.

Leah was my Hebrew name, my heritage. I was a descendant of our tribe from a shtetl in eastern Europe, whose offspring had fled the pogroms and found their way as immigrants to Johannesburg, South Africa. I was a Jew. I could not sing the praises of Jesus, so I kept my mouth shut tight and hoped that no one would notice, while Abraham, Isaac, and Moses watched me from above. "Yes, Jesus loves me, the Bible tells me so!" Hundreds of voices sang the final chorus. And I was alone in my silence.

As we filed out of the pristine auditorium, I was relieved that I had managed to keep my singing secret safe for one more school assembly. I was eight years old, and there were hundreds more weekly school assemblies to come, but I tried not to think about them. As I put on my shoes and tied the one with the shorter lace into a less-than-perfect bow, I wondered why my parents hadn't sent me and my sisters to King David, where all my cousins went. But my mother and father were not the sort to send their kids to such a school. My parents were Jews of the delicatessen kind, heavy on noodle kugel and gefilte fish, but light on the Talmud and Torah. My father's beliefs centered on things that were grounded in the earth. He was pious about politics and religious about smoking two packs of cigarettes a day, Rothman's filtered, which he couldn't be without. My mother mentioned God only when she was in front of her vanity table. "Oh God, I've glued these false eyelashes on backward!" She mentioned

Jesus, too, mostly on the tennis court. "Jesus Christ, I can't believe I missed that shot!"

There was only one sign in our home that we were of the Hebrew tribe — those who had wandered in the desert for forty years — and it was a mezuzah placed on the doorpost to the entrance of our home. A little rectangular box, it contained the first verses of the Torah on parchment in Hebrew, I was told by my cousin Merlyn, who went to King David. They learned that kind of stuff at her school, she had told me proudly. I was always eager to hurry my best friend, Mary Waite, with the wispy blonde hair and blue eyes, through the front door when she came over to play, for fear she would notice the ancient scroll on the doorpost.

God was not ever discussed in our home, and I knew Jesus probably didn't want anything to do with the dark-haired little girl who refused to sing his praises in school assembly at Parkview Junior School in the suburbs of Johannesburg below. I was spiritually rudderless. So, while my father ranted on about the state of the world, blowing smoke and leaving its stale trail through the house, and my mother floated from tennis games to lunches, leaving lipstick stains on glasses and the scent of her spicy perfume mingling with the odor of his tobacco, I held on to fluff and fur.

My savior was four legged, black and marmalade in color, with big green eyes. His name was Yoyo. He purred the loudest and licked the softest of any cat I had ever known. When doors were slammed and voices loud and shrill from my parents' bedroom down the hall, I did not pray to something above to make the fighting stop. Instead I held on tightly to Yoyo's soft, long-haired coat. That was all the comfort that I needed. Yoyo never squirmed under my grasp; he seemed to know to relax and let me draw whatever it was that I needed from him. I had gotten him as a kitten two years earlier from a woman who made dresses for my mother. The dressmaker's cat had given birth to five, and I chose him without hesitation: big green eyes that filled me up with liquid warmth immediately. I had the joy of Yoyo in my life for two and a half years. I experienced all that was good and pure in his small warm body and was given holy love, unwavering and unconditional.

ON THE MORNING THAT STARTED LIKE ANY OTHER and ended like no other, I remember Yoyo playing with the laces of my shoes that were never allowed in assembly. "We'll play in the garden, when I come home. I promise," I said, as I kissed him quickly on his pink nose. And we did, for most of that afternoon until the sun was almost gone, in the mauve light tinged with the last rays of gold. I had climbed the big plum tree and Yoyo had followed me up, meowing and rubbing against my arm. Then helter-skelter, down he went. I stayed sitting in the tree's cool branches, sucking on a plum, the juice sweet and smooth on my tongue. Then a bark and a snarl followed by a hideous strangled meow reached my ears through the foliage. I leaned forward quickly, so I could see all the way to the edge of our property line, the place where the awful sound had come from. I almost toppled down by the vision of the shocking, horrible scene on the far side of the garden. Yoyo had his head pulled through the chain-linked fence. On the other side was Morgan, the dog that lived next door. He was viciously pulling and pulling on my beloved cat. "NO! NO! NO!" I screamed. I flew down the tree and raced across the lawn, a mother bird on a mission to save its young. I kicked and kicked at Morgan through the spaces in the linked fence until he let go, his mouth dripping red.

I picked up a limp-bodied Yoyo and carried him in my arms across the lawn. The air was cooler now. The light gone. Time moved very slowly and the journey across the lawn felt endless. I was numb and cold but with a single thought in my head. My cat was going to be fine.

I laid Yoyo down on the linoleum kitchen floor and opened a can of cat food. My hands shook. My mouth was dry and my pulse raced with hope.

"Eat, you'll be better. Please stand up, Yoyo, and eat." But Yoyo didn't move.

I pleaded. I prayed for the first time in my life. "Dear God, please let my cat live. I promise I'll have a bat mitzvah when I'm thirteen. I'll call myself Leah from now on."

But Yoyo didn't move.

"Jesus," I pleaded, "I'll sing. I promise, I'll be the loudest in assembly with the sweetest voice of all."

But still, Yoyo didn't move.

"Please, Yoyo. Please. Just take one small taste." I put the cat food into the palm of my hand and held it to his bloody mouth.

My nanny, Nellie, came in and saw me kneeling over the cat I loved so much, the can of salmon cat food smeared all over my hands. "He is dead, Miss Lin," she said. "Come," she held her rounded arms out to me, and I ran into them and wept.

Out back, where the corn grew high and the chickens ran free and wild, I buried Yoyo. Thomas, the gardener, dug the grave, and I found the box that my school shoes had come in at the back of my closet. Inside was a brand new pair of laces, so I buried them with Yoyo. I knew he would like that. My parents offered to get me a new kitten, but I said no. There was only one cat for me, and he never was to be replaced.

SIX MONTHS PASSED, and I had become even smaller than I already was. My clothes, baggy and ill fitting, looked like they belonged to a rosier, more robust child. Nothing felt right, nothing tasted good, and going to sleep at night was the hardest of all. I did not have Yoyo's soft fur to wrap around my wounds. The thing I believed in most was gone.

While my father still chain-smoked and my mother still drifted in and out of the house, I became fixated with thoughts of Yoyo and what he looked like now. One swelteringly hot summer afternoon, when I could stand it no more, I took a shovel from the cool dark coal shed and went to find out. Deeper and deeper I dug, my hair matted and wet from the solo exertion of exhuming my beloved cat. When metal finally hit the cardboard box I had buried him in, I whispered his name. "Yoyo, I'm here." But when I opened the box, it released a stench so strong that it made my stomach lurch, and bile filled my parched throat. Inside were bits of bone and tufts of fur. Maggots crawled everywhere, but something inside me willed me to keep looking. The earth around the remains was thick and tarlike, transformed, it seemed, by his lifeless form. Small white worms crawled through the

black and orange fur that I had clung to so often. But somehow I got past the shock of the stench. I willed myself to not
be sick. I needed to be here, with my cat. Then suddenly, I
did not feel repulsed or revolted anymore. A calmness came
over me. I stood in the garden for a long, long time, just staring at his remains. I did not care that the unforgiving sun
was burning my shoulders, or that my head throbbed and
my arms ached from my exertions with a heavy shovel. I felt
something opening and closing inside me all at once. I bent
down and clutched the putrid earth in my bare hands, knowing it was just that. Earth.

I was now ready to begin the task of closing the grave.
As I shoveled dirt, I knew that all I was covering was bones
and fur, not my beloved cat. Yoyo was long gone. Joined
with the savior, as he had once been a savior for me. Now
they were one.

Something inside me shifted that day. I no longer hurried my friend Mary Waite through the front door past the
mezuzah. In fact, I showed it to her when she next came
over. "There's a Hebrew scroll inside," I told her, pointing
toward the symbol of our faith. "My family is Jewish, you
know." She punched me in the arm. "Silly, of course I knew.
That's why my mom never serves ham or bacon when you
come over."

In school assembly the next week, I opened my mouth
and sang, "Yes, Jesus loves me. Yes, Jesus loves me. Yes, Jesus
loves me. The Bible tells me so." My voice was strong and
clear, my mouth a perfect O. I knew that up in the heavens

they wouldn't be angry at me. I figured anything that powerful would not get hung up on what they were called.

When assembly was over, I sat and tied my shoes, the ones with the one shorter lace. I knew it didn't matter anymore if my name was Linzi or Leah, or whether I was Jewish or Christian. I felt a rush of Yoyo inside me, that same liquid warmth I had felt the first time I laid eyes on him. And, as I followed the throng of kids out into the bright morning sun, God, Abraham, Isaac, Moses, Jesus, and Yoyo smiled down on me from above.

15.

MY SAL

Jacqueline Winspear

I put down the phone and walked into my husband's office — we both work from home — where Sally, our almost-fifteen-year-old black Lab, lay resting, along with the cat, on one of several beds we had placed around the house for her. She lifted her head as I sat down beside her, her eyes milky with age, her muzzle gray, and she smiled. Yes, she smiled.

"I made the appointment. Scott said to come at four forty-five."

John stopped working and leaned forward to rub Sal's head. "Let's all go sit in the garden," he said.

We spent almost all day in the garden, the four of us shaded by the walnut tree in late-September sun. Deldy, our calico cat, would not leave Sal's side, and Sal would not leave mine; we had thirteen years of history and a compendium of memories — sweet, good, and bad — behind us.

I WAS SINGLE AND LIVING IN THE MARIN COUNTY town of San Anselmo when I decided I wanted to have a dog again. I was brought up in rural Kent, in England, and because we'd had dogs ever since I could remember, a home without a dog seemed an empty home indeed. My studio apartment — the top floor of a family home where my landlords lived — also had a large deck and another room on the opposite side, so I had a fair bit of space. I thought that, with morning saunters, evening walks, and weekend hikes up to Mount Tam, the prospective new dog would have plenty of room and exercise. The first hurdle was in gaining the permission of my landlords, Christopher and Sabrina. I stopped them one day when they'd just returned from an outing with their two young sons — Nate was six at the time, and Matthew four. I waited until the boys had run into the house; the last thing I wanted was to use the emotional blackmail of children who wanted a dog.

"Um, I wonder if I could ask you something — and really, I know this is a big one, and I really, really understand if you say no, so…"

They looked at me, their smiles frozen in anticipation of my request.

"Well, I've been thinking, I would really like a dog and — "

The smiles grew broader; Sabrina beamed. "Oh, Jackie, of course you can — that's wonderful!" She leaned around the door. "Hey — Nate! Matthew! Jackie's getting a dog!"

The boys came running out as if the prospective canine were in the driveway, ready for inspection. Questions came thick and fast — when would the dog come home? What sort of dog? Could they play with him — or her?

I went along to the Humane Society the next day and made my application. I was clear about the type of dog I wanted — medium to large, but not giant; house-trained; good temperament; excellent with kids; and generally an all-around nice dog. And though there were dogs I could have taken home in a heartbeat, it would be a while before I found "the one." The boys took to waiting in the driveway for me to come home.

"Why haven't you got a dog yet?" Matthew asked one day, crestfallen that the long-awaited four-legged one was not with me.

"We're all waiting," added Christopher, joining the boys.

"I know. I'll find one soon."

It was on February 14th that I made another trip to the Humane Society, sighing as I walked alongside the cages with dogs jumping up for attention. "Choose me, choose me, I'm a good dog," they seemed to be saying. I reached a cage where there was a new dog in residence, but no dog to be seen. I took her rap sheet from its holder on the outside of the run — the fact that it was there meant that she was not out with a prospective owner — and read the short history, and behaviorist's assessment. "Two years old...loves to walk...good with children and other dogs...not possessive with food." Then, "this dog does not know how to play."

Each dog had a long narrow run, divided in the center by a concrete wall to separate the animal's living space from its personal viewing area. A small archway allowed the dog to go to and fro; possibly the designer had the idea in mind that the dog could go back beyond the archway to the living space if it needed some peace and quiet. On this day, all the other dogs were not about to miss a chance and were firmly up front to be viewed — but where was this dog? I knelt down to look through the archway, to see if she was there. And in that moment, a shy black Labrador with a bright white tuxedo chest was craning her neck, curious to see who might have stopped to look for her. I smiled.

"Hello, you," I said.

And if a dog could smile, then she smiled the widest smile I have ever seen. She trotted toward me, sat in front of the wire, and put up one paw to touch my hand. I looked around for a helper.

"Can I take this dog for a walk?"

THE FOLLOWING DAY, Christopher, Sabrina, Nate, and Matthew were waiting outside the house when I drove in, with Sally riding shotgun. She passed her first test with flying colors — the boys were all over her and she just lapped it up. Sabrina hugged Sal to her chest, and I thought for a moment I'd lost my new dog.

I knew the first month would be the most challenging for Sal, so she came to work with me for a while. Luckily, I was a sales rep at the time, so I could organize my schedule to allow Sally to spend increasing amounts of time on her own, until she was happy to spend most of the day sleeping on the deck, or in my home office — as long as we had that morning walk and play, and a long hike late afternoon. We met new friends on the morning walk — Nina and her dog, Blaze, and Ellen and Bandit. The three dogs became best buddies, their morning romp together forming part of the ritual that helped turn Sal from a good dog into a great dog. But our early days together were not without problems.

It was during a routine vaccination visit to the vet — she'd been with me for about a month — that I expressed a concern that Sal was "depressed."

"She plays now, and loves to run with the ball. But sometimes I look at her, and it's as if she's really down, you know, like someone who can't forget a bad experience. I take her to the park to cheer her up, but, well..."

Dr. Rob Erteman, Sally's vet in San Anselmo, nodded, looking into her eyes, and stroking her head. "Jackie, though animals don't remember in the same way that you and I remember, there are things that have happened to them — especially rescue dogs — that have caused them pain. And just like our bad experiences don't just go away, neither do a dog's." He paused; Sally leaned in toward him. "Now, if one of your friends comes over to tell you about something bad that's happened, you don't say, 'Let's go play!' Instead you put your arm around her, you reassure her, and you tell her you're there for her. And that's what you have to do with Sal. Every day, in a quiet time, tell her that you love her — and tell her she's safe. She'll understand."

So, that evening, after our walk and dinner, I sat on the floor, my back against the sofa, and held out my hand for Sally to come to me. She snuggled into the crook of my arm, her head resting against my chest.

"You're safe now, Sally," I said. "I will never leave you. You're mine. I will always love you, and I'll take care of you forever."

Within a week, another, more vibrant Sally emerged. Even the light in her eyes seemed brighter. And she proved that she really knew how to play!

SALLY ALSO KNEW HOW TO HAVE ACCIDENTS. Rob Erteman commented on one occasion that he could even set his watch by her forays into emergency veterinary medicine — they always seemed to happen late on a Friday afternoon, just at the point when he thought there was only one more patient to see before the weekend. These accidents varied, from a run-in with barbed wire, to an overindulgence in swimming that left her with too much water in her gut; there was the fall down a twenty-five-foot wall, and the day she had her side ripped open by the big black dog whose owner never seemed to be around at the park. On that occasion I raced her down to the animal hospital in the car, then ran into the packed waiting room only to find I could not speak. Dr. Erteman's receptionist, Tink, looked at me and realized I was in shock.

"It's Sally?" she prompted.

I nodded.

"She's hurt — badly?"

I nodded.

"Bring her in right away — I'll tell Dr. Erteman. Do you need help?"

I shook my head and ran out to the car, helping Sal to walk in under her own steam while dripping blood across the waiting room floor on her way to the examination room. I turned around to nod my thanks to everyone in the waiting room — they'd be there for a while now. Rob Erteman lifted

Sally straight up onto the metal table. Jill, the veterinary nurse, helped to hold her while Rob inspected the wound. A boy from the local high school on work experience stood next to me as I watched the vet's expression; I was looking for a sign that everything would be all right.

"OK, if anyone's going to faint — " He looked at me, then the teenager. "You'd better leave now."

"I'll be fine," I said.

The boy nodded. I think we both felt a bit queasy.

I hugged Sally's head to my chest as Rob set to work.

"It's OK, Sal," I whispered. "You're safe — I won't leave you."

WHEN I FIRST MET JOHN, we talked about our dogs. He had joint custody of his dog, Spike, with his former wife, and I told him all about my Sal, who was now five years old. I always said that John fell in love with Sally long before he fell for me; when he walked into the house and called out, "Where's my girl?" I knew I wasn't the girl in question.

We moved to Ojai when Sally was eight, and soon afterward my travel schedule increased. My first two books had been published, and long book tours demanded weeks away from home. I was also trying to get back to the United Kingdom several times each year to visit my now-elderly parents. During that time John and Sally grew closer and kept each other company, joined by Delderfield, the cat who adopted us as soon as we moved into our new home. Sally and Deldy had become inseparable; where one went, the other followed.

A routine dental exam when Sally was eleven years old led to the discovery of an aggressive mouth cancer. I received the news on the evening before I was due to fly back to England to see my parents — my mother had suffered a minor stroke earlier in the year, so those visits had taken on a greater significance. I was going to cancel the trip, but John insisted that everything would be fine. While I was in the air, Dr. Scott Smith, our vet in Carpinteria, would be operating on Sally — neither the trip nor the surgery could wait. I remember sitting on that plane, looking out at the black night sky. I prayed. *Give me one more year with her, just one more year.*

JOHN SAID IT WAS JUST AS WELL I was in England when Sally came out of the hospital; she was so very ill. He turned his attention to being her full-time caregiver for the following week, until I could stand the distance no longer and flew home early. He was hand-feeding Sally at this stage and had designed a special drinking fountain because she was unable to lap her water. Soon she was able to eat wet food from a plate on her own — the ideal plate was a faux silver platter I'd found at a garage sale for seventy-five cents — and we both cherished our special time in the evening when she would sit in the crook of my arm while I told her she was safe and loved. With her recovery in progress, we decided that every day had to be a banner day for Sally, and if the banner days became few and far between, then we would do what was best for her. Above all, she would not be allowed to suffer.

Those banner days became good days for us too. We met new friends at the local park; we'd finish work early to take Sal to the beach; or perhaps we'd just go for a coffee downtown, sit outside, and watch the world go by. Sally became a grande dame of doghood, those many accidents of her earlier years coming home to roost and slowing her down — but I had asked for a year and had been given three.

Sally — aka Sally Wagster, Wagerooni, Wagatha Labsy, Sally-Sue — lay on the ground between us as we sat in the garden and talked about her life, remembering her speed at the dog park, her love of the water — *what about when she tried to swim to Japan from Montara Beach* — those accidents. And the fact that she would have sold her soul for roast chicken — *hey, remember when she chased that hen? And remember when we found her — all of her — foraging in the trash can?*

Oh, remember when . . . remember when . . . remember when . . .

And then it was four-fifteen. Time to leave.

"We'd better get going," said John.

We helped her into the car, leaving Deldy on the porch to await our return.

As if she knew this was her final journey, Sal's breathing became labored on the way to the animal hospital. I held her close. "I'm with you, my love, I'm here."

We lifted her out of the car, and though she was still breathing with difficulty, she stumbled over to the grass and relieved herself as if she were determined not to cause embarrassment inside the hospital. Her dignity maintained, she could walk no further, so John and Scott Smith carried her inside and laid her on the examining table.

"Not a second too soon, or a moment too late — she's crashing, and probably wouldn't last the night," said Dr. Smith.

The veterinary nurse, Regina, pressed a small silver angel dog into my hand, and tears filled her eyes. Yes, everyone loved Sal.

I turned away as Dr. Smith prepared the syringe, then leaned forward and rested my head next to Sally's while John rubbed her back. Dr. Smith explained what would happen, that after he'd administered the injection, Sally would just pass away as if falling into a deep sleep.

"I'll leave you alone with her, then come back later to make sure."

I held Sally closer. "I'm here, Sal. I love you, girl. You're safe now; I won't leave you..."

Scott Smith slipped the needle into her foreleg and lowered the lights. Within seconds her breathing calmed, the heavy rasping stopped. And I whispered the words "I love you, my Sal" one last time.

16.

KIKI

Cecilia Manguerra Brainard

When Chintzy, our male cat, died at age nineteen, Fraidy, the white cat, settled down to be our only pet. She had always been a dour cat, used to being a second banana all her life, and she seemed surprised at the attention she had never experienced before. She was enjoying her new status and would now jump up on our laps when we watched TV and even dared sleep on our bed at night, a privilege that Chintzy had made exclusively his.

My husband, too, made adjustments to our new pet situation. "That's it! Just one cat, no more." He knew more about cats than I did. I had grown up with German shepherds for pets; our cats had been relegated to catching rats and lizards outside. He was the one who had wanted cats, not dogs. "Cats," he said, "are more independent and don't need as much care and attention as dogs do. For one thing, they know when to stop eating, unlike dogs, who'll finish all the food you give them." It was true that we could go away on weekends and leave food and water for our cats and they'd be just fine. But overall, I found our cats to be aloof, demanding, somewhat arrogant creatures, unlike the exuberant dogs of my youth who had pounced on me when I returned home from school, and who had followed me around, begging for attention.

Soon after my husband's decision to have only one cat, our eldest son, Chris, showed up holding a kitten just six weeks old. "Can she stay here for a little while?" he asked us. He had broken up with his girlfriend and was moving soon. The kitten was a long-haired tuxedo cat, with black fur down her back and white on her belly; part of her face was white; she had a crooked black mustache and was scrawny and a female to boot.

"We've decided we want only one cat," my husband told Chris, "and you know we prefer male cats with short hair. Female cats are bitchy — remember Grandma Dinah's Siamese that would piss on her clothes when she got mad? And long-haired cats shed, and they have fleas..."

Chris handed the black-and-white kitten to his father; it was so small it fit the palm of his hand.

"We just got rid of one cat; we don't want another one." The kitten crawled up his arm and made her way up to his neck. "And look at this long black fur." She started to lick his cheek. "Well," he said in a softer voice, "just until you get settled, and then you can pick her up."

That never happened, of course. Kiki (a name given by the girlfriend) entered our lives when my husband and I were in our middle age and Chris was leaving for law school, our middle son was in college, and the youngest was in high school. It was a busy household with a very upset white cat who probably had hoped she would be the only cat, and who now looked at the black-and-white kitten as an unwelcome interloper.

Kiki, on the other hand, perked up when she saw Fraidy and quickly headed for her belly, wanting to suckle. Fraidy, a virgin cat without an ounce of maternal instinct in her, hissed and swiped her with a paw. Kiki tried again and again, and the white cat became hysterical, growling and carrying on until finally the kitten got the message and left her alone. For a couple of days the two cats avoided each other. But later on I saw Kiki sneak up on Fraidy, who was sunning herself on the fourth step of the spiral staircase. Kiki reached up and grabbed her tail, setting off another cat fight. Kiki took to waiting behind doors and pouncing on Fraidy, which left her even more frazzled, more nervous.

Kiki learned to be the perfect pet. When you picked her up, she purred loudly and snuggled up against you, thoroughly content. She would even bat your face with her paw, a friendly tap, as if to say, "Hi, there."

She slept on our bed and, on cold nights, would crawl under the blanket to lie right next to me. She never resisted when I held her tight, and I did this often because I hated cold nights and Kiki was warm like a furry hot-water bag. She would wait a few minutes until she thought I was asleep, and then she would carefully disentangle herself and return to the exact spot I had picked her up from.

In the early morning, she would jump off our bed and run downstairs and out the cat door to do her business. Then her day began. She had breakfast; outside she would sit in the sun and groom herself — on what used to be Fraidy's favorite sunning spot, the fourth step of the spiral staircase. In the spring, when there were many sparrows about, she'd catch birds and drag them into the house. She never killed them, and despite my hysterics over the flapping birds, she would continue to do this until the last spring of her life. In the afternoon, she moved back into the house to nap on the couch in the den or on our bed. In between all these activities, she'd search out Fraidy to bat her tail or whack her behind. In the evening, when we were watching TV in the den, she would climb up on my husband's lap to sleep or play. They could sit quietly on the chair for hours, my husband doing the crossword puzzle or Sudoku and Kiki napping. "She loves you," I would tell him. He'd shrug and say, "She's a cat, she uses people."

Meanwhile, Fraidy took to spending most of her time in our neighbor's yard. One day, our neighbor called to ask if our white cat was depressed, because she spent most of her time sunning herself on their dog's marked grave.

Fraidy developed cancer on her ears, and the vet explained that this often happened to white cats, since they had no melanin to protect them from the ultraviolet rays of the sun — just like humans. Fraidy developed black spots on her ears that turned into ugly sores. The vet lopped off most of her ears. "You must put sunblock on her ears and nose if she goes outside. In fact, it would be better if you kept her indoors."

We decided to turn our master bedroom upstairs into Fraidy's room, and put her litter box and food and water in the bathroom. She had a sleeping pad on the bedroom floor, and her sleeping blanket on our bed. We left the bedroom door closed to keep her in and Kiki out. I nursed Fraidy in our bedroom for the next four years. She thrived on this arrangement.

Kiki, however, was furious she had been driven away from our/her bedroom. One didn't have to be a pet psychologist to know that Kiki was angry and jealous that her nemesis had the most important room in the house. She must have blamed me for her exile from the bedroom, because she turned cool toward me, preferring my husband instead. She didn't hiss at me or resist when I picked her up, but for the longest time she wouldn't purr. And she made no eye contact with me. When my husband held her, her purring could be heard throughout the house — as if she were saying, "I love him, I love him...but not you."

YEARS LATER, LONG AFTER FRAIDY WAS GONE, I would look at Kiki and think, *You and I are getting old.* She started having difficulty jumping on our bed; sometimes she limped; she spent more time napping; and she would nip your hand if you touched her lower back the wrong way. But she always remained playful.

Chris had become a lawyer by now, and he moved near us with his new girlfriend, who wanted a cat. My husband, who constantly dreamed of simplifying our lives, volunteered to return Kiki, and they took her to their two-bedroom apartment. Kiki peed inside their shoes and on their clothes, including the leather jacket of the girlfriend, who, fortunately, laughed it off. Our son was not so good-natured, and one day he burst into our kitchen holding Kiki. Hands shaking, he handed her to us and said, "Take her, or else I'll take her to the pound!" Unfazed Kiki sauntered to the den, jumped up on the couch, and began grooming herself. She looked smug, as if thinking, *This is where I want to live. Don't ever try to change my life again.*

But changes did come. Kiki's life revolved around our house and garden and a bit of the neighborhood — a small planet. The neighbors' cats came and went; she had one cat friend who was also a tuxedo cat, but older; one day he stopped coming around. She watched Fraidy take the last trip to the vet. Kiki saw our house evolve: a bedroom becoming an office, the front yard acquiring a gate. She watched my husband and me gain weight, begin moving more slowly, and start talking about doctors and dentists more. She watched our three sons grow taller, and saw them come and go as they went to college, returned home, found work, lost a job, fell in love, fell out of love, or got married. And throughout all this, Kiki was a fixture for all of us, the one thing permanent in our lives.

She disliked the grandchildren; she did not like children touching her. The sudden uncontrolled movements of the young ones made her nervous. When she saw them coming, she would shudder with disgust and run off to hide in the garden or upstairs in our bedroom. This did not discourage the grandchildren's awe, and they would shout excitedly when they saw her: "Look, Kiki's here!" as if she were a unicorn, a rare and beautiful creature.

At one point, our ages were the same, mine in human years, hers in cat years. Her black fur had faded and picked up a reddish tint; my dyed black hair had done the same. I felt there was a bond between us, and it was a bond that went deeper than the color of our hair or fur. One night the bed was too high for her, and she fell when she jumped up. We found a footstool to help her. She had gum and tooth problems, and I ignored the vet's suggestion to have all her teeth pulled out. She healed, and still had enough teeth to bite you with if you stroked her the wrong way.

She still preferred my husband's lap to mine until the very end, but she knew she could rely on me. I was the one who took her to the veterinarian, who Googled her illnesses, who popped pills into her mouth, who brushed her thick black fur, who cleaned her remaining little teeth with a finger contraption, who gave her mercury-free people tuna or bits of steak, who cajoled her into drinking water when she was very ill. It was difficult to watch her grow old, like watching myself heading down the same path. And the fact of it was that Kiki had become so much a part of my life and myself that I couldn't imagine not having her around. Even her naughtiness and arrogance had become lovable. I realized I loved this cat.

Sometime during the seventeen years we had her, a reversal of roles took place. Kiki ceased being our pet who tried to please us; she became the master, and we her servants who tried hard to please her, or at least I did. Until the end I was her nurse and secretary, jotting down her imagined missives in a blog, as if giving her voice would make her live a little bit longer, just a bit longer, even when she would look at me pleadingly as if to say, "Let me go. Stop forcing me to drink water and eat. I'm tired."

SHE WOULD SPEND HOURS IN THE ROSE GARDEN under the bougainvillea bush, where she could watch and listen to the birds and squirrels. She stopped sleeping on our bed, preferring the den couch. Perhaps climbing up on the bed became a nuisance; perhaps being close to us, being touched by us, became an annoyance. She retreated from us and communed with nature.

One gorgeous spring day, Kiki was out in the rose garden — a black-and-white cat lying contentedly under the bougainvillea covered with brilliant red flowers. The rose bushes displayed huge blooms of red, yellow, and pink. I could hear the birds twittering in the bougainvillea. I had done all I could for her, including carrying her in my arms and whispering affirmations: *You can do it. You'll be well again. You have to eat. You have to drink so you'll live.* That day, Kiki was comfortable and happy in her rose garden. I went to my office to work. Then suddenly I heard a meow, and when I looked up I saw Kiki enter my office. She had something in her mouth — a baby bird, which she dropped in front of me. I jumped up; the fluttering of the birds always upset me. Kiki looked straight at me; she had an expression, something in her eyes. I realized the baby bird was her gift to me. I picked her up, hugged her tight. "Thank you," I said.

Three months later we buried her in her beloved rose garden, next to the bougainvillea bush.

17.

WONDER DOG

Victoria Zackheim

When my husband moved out, our children were confused, frightened, and desperately unhappy. As much as I tried to soothe their hearts, their emotions ran deep. One afternoon, in a moment of what was either brilliance or foolishness, I took my son, age eleven, to a local pet store. Matthew immediately fell for a tiny Australian shepherd mix (the salesperson swore the dog would grow to perhaps fifteen pounds...ha!), and we agreed that a little black puffball of a cockapoo was perfect for his sister, age nine. When we presented the puppy to Alisa, she let out a little shriek of surprise and then melted with pleasure. By the end of the day, Matthew was the caretaker of Pookie, and Alisa was devoting every ounce of maternal instinct to the cuddly mass she had named Muffy. I watched the children with their new pets, saw the joy and tenderness in their faces, and knew with certainty that, no matter how much work these puppies would require, they would bring joy to my children.

Four years later, Matthew was fourteen and living with his father, and Alisa had moved with me to a turn-of-the-century craftsman-style home in Palo Alto. The old house was nearly perfect; the only drawback was the backyard. While it was more than large enough for trees, flowers, and a vegetable garden, it was inadequate for the needs of what had become a very large Pookie — a full-sized dog whose need to run far exceeded the space. At the time, Matthew's father was unable to keep the dog, so we were left with a terrible decision — what to do about Pookie, one of the most loving and intelligent dogs who ever existed. With a deep sense that I was letting down my son, I gave Pookie to a woman who had long admired and adored him. The fact that she lived on more than an acre of doggie playground did not assuage my guilt.

I had decided to make the move to the active and education-focused Palo Alto, from the sleepy Los Gatos community at the foot of the Santa Cruz Mountains, because I believed Alisa would thrive in this new and culturally rich environment. I was wrong. Adolescence was not easy for my daughter. Here we were, in a town where she knew no one, yet she soldiered on through middle school. When she entered high school, she was charming and beautiful, and made many new friends, but I became overly protective and too often distrusted her choices. We argued incessantly. Was she really going to wear *that* to school? (Glare.) Did she have any intention of doing her homework? (Roll eyes.) Was it asking too much to meet this girl's family before my baby climbed into that car and disappeared into parts unknown? (Slam door.) There were times when I questioned whether my daughter, or even her mother, would survive these years, and I sought counsel about being a better mother, more accepting, less controlling.

As I floundered and gasped through the process, often leaving my daughter wondering what the hell her mother was trying to convey or accomplish, there was one constant in her life that never, ever let her down. Never forgot to love her. Never turned away and sighed too loudly when she was in the throes of one of those teenage pique or angst moments. That constant was Muffy, the sweetest dog, the most steadfast companion. I recall telling my friends that Muffy was my protector as well, because, had my daughter ever been armed, she would never have pulled the trigger for fear that the bullet might pass through my heart, hit the wall, deflect off a pipe, and somehow find its way to Muffy!

Imagine, if you will, a girl of fifteen, tall and coltish, a mass of auburn hair tumbling around a face that, only a year earlier, was notable for the braces she wore on her teeth. Suddenly she was duckling-to-swan beautiful. My daughter was bighearted and kind, unaware of her beauty, and yet she suspected that something was indeed changing. Now imagine a girl typically confused, wondering where her life was going, too young to imagine more than a few days into the future. Was she afraid? Did her world feel unsafe? I wanted only to protect her, to provide a haven where she never had to question whether she was accepted and loved. I didn't always succeed.

Filling in the gaps was Muffy, a fluffball of a dog who would race into her room, jump on her bed, use his nose to lift the covers, then rush down to her feet, where he would promptly turn around, scoot back up toward the light, and, in a show of devotion and uncanny — but perhaps not un-canine — perception, plop his head on the pillow, look into this girl's eyes, and give her one slurpy lick on the face. After sighing in unison, they would fall asleep. And those times when my beautiful woman/child picked up Muffy and hugged him? He would place both paws on her shoulders and return the hug. Thanks to this dog, the confusions of adolescence were less painful.

There was a time when, for many long and difficult months, my daughter had to share Muffy's tender nature with me, a mother going through her own angst. I had fallen in love with a smart, quirky man who was, alas, emotion-ally unavailable — a recurring theme in my life — and the collapse of this relationship left me bereft. (Actually, miles beyond bereft, but *gasping for air* or *falling into a useless and pathetic mass of protoplasm* seem melodramatic, accurate as these phrases might be.) I worked all day, nagged Alisa about her homework and responsibilities all evening, and then cried myself to sleep. My poor daughter was torn between keeping her own head above water and making certain her mother's life jacket was securely fastened. Enter Muffy. In addition to being my daughter's loving support, the dog who may have understood nothing about teenage challenges and brokenhearted women somehow keenly sensed the need for his loving presence. With Muffy nearby, both of us felt adored and appreciated.

ALISA WAS NEARLY EIGHTEEN and about to graduate and head off to university when disaster struck. After a weekend away, we came home to find Muffy on my bed, his curled-up body surrounded by feces. I was furious and shouted at him to jump down, which he did. Rather than racing into the kitchen and out the doggy door as usual, he scuttled along the floor, back legs dragging behind him. Alisa and I rushed him to a local vet, where they kept him overnight for observation. The next day, they informed us that he had ruptured a vertebra and nothing could be done: the paralysis was permanent.

We were faced with a weighty decision. The vet told us that surgery was purposeless, but what if there was even a smidgen of hope? Certainly the dog who had given his all to our family deserved every chance at recovery. We spoke to several veterinarians and learned that a clinic in Santa Cruz specialized in the kind of spinal surgery that sometimes reversed a dog's paralysis. We made an appointment and murmured hopeful incantations.

After the surgery we brought Muffy home. Over the next few weeks, we tended to his wound and kept him comfortable. I took him onto the lawn several times each day and performed acupressure on his bladder, because he was no longer able to empty it on his own. He always looked away, as if embarrassed that a life of joyful dashing about had somehow come to this. Were we expecting too much from him and selfishly trying to convince ourselves that he could live a happy life on two legs? Ambulatory or not, Muffy would continue to dispense unlimited love, but at what price?

I rigged a sling for his midsection and walked him around the neighborhood, his hind legs dangling above the ground and his front legs racing as if nothing had changed. A veterinarian who specialized in acupuncture came to the house and inserted needles into areas that energized nerves. We bought a wheeled contraption that, when strapped on, took the place of his paralyzed legs. Sadly, nothing changed the fact that, when Muffy was not harnessed, or his legs were not supported, those legs dragged behind him like boneless flesh. Even worse, he became quiet and withdrawn.

The day finally arrived when we had to accept the truth. With Alisa now a young adult and her mother finally getting the hang of motherhood, we were able to talk this through, share our sense of impending grief, and give each other the emotional support required to make the right decision.

On the appointed day, we drove back over the Santa Cruz Mountains for the postsurgical evaluation. Alisa carried Muffy into the waiting room and held him close. The evaluation took only minutes, and we were told that, as we had feared, his injury was too severe, that nothing had changed.

Alisa and I were left alone to confer. We both knew what had to be done, but the choice was beyond painful. We held each other, Muffy between us licking our faces as we wept over what we both knew to be the inevitable. As the doctor and his assistant assembled syringe and vial, we cradled our dog, stroking him and speaking with love. We thanked him for the years of joy he had brought into our lives and wished him a life where he could run freely and without pain. With Alisa holding his head and murmuring to him, and me scratching him behind the ears and wishing him a peaceful journey, he died quietly.

I loved that dog. Even when he rushed up to me, rolled over to have his tummy scratched, and piddled every damn time, he was special. The fact that he died more than twenty years ago and his memory can still evoke such emotions says so much about the role he played in our lives. There's a joke that has to do with the question of when life begins. Three clerics are arguing the point. The priest insists that life begins at conception, while the minister states that life begins at birth. The rabbi announces, "Life begins when the children go off to college and the dog dies." Muffy's death was not a new beginning but the end of a period in our lives that had been fraught with tension and uncertainty, teenage confusion, and a mother's need to control. It was also a time when love and acceptance, warmth and joy, were delivered by a fluffy little dog who reminded my daughter every day that she was lovable, that she mattered, and that no matter how difficult life seemed, no matter how much she felt that her well-intentioned mother was making a botch of mothering, he was always there to share her pillow, listen to her secrets ... and never tell.

18

MY VIRTUAL CAT

Jenny Rough

I found a silky white cat in my inbox. She was a long-haired
Persian mix, and as soon as I clicked on her photo, I knew
we'd be a good match. She had been abandoned at a veterinarian's office, the same place my friend Suz took her dog.
The cat was sixteen years old, and she peed — a lot (early
stage kidney disease, not yet fatal). Suz sent the sob story out
into cyberspace with an announcement that the cat needed a
new home. Icy was pure white except for her nose, pink as a
cherry blossom, and cloudy blue eyes that sat buried in her
furry face.

"Adorable, adorable," I typed back to Suz. "I'll take her."

All I had to do was convince Ron.

Ron inherited my dog when we married, a Lab mix.
He embraced her from the start — hiding treats behind
her water dish as a surprise, buying a retractable leash so
she could trot ten feet ahead of us down the sidewalk, and

spending Saturday afternoons tossing a soft Frisbee for her at the park. Even though he welcomed her, he believed a dog deserved a yard. We didn't have a yard. Instead, Ron and I kept moving from one rental to another (apartments, condos, row houses). He was ready to plunk down our savings to buy a home near Washington, D.C., where we lived, but my dream was to return to California, the place we met and married. Not yet ready to sever my ties out west, I frequently flew back and forth between coasts. This would pose a problem if we took in a new cat. While I could assume the bulk of responsibilities most of the time — litter box, food, vet appointments — when I left town I'd be pawning Icy off on him. If Ron was okay with the plan, we'd be fine. But I had my suspicions.

It's not that we didn't want to grow our family. There *was* a barren space in our home (rather, our town home). But the missing piece wasn't a feline. It was a child. Three years earlier, I'd had a miscarriage. The loss occurred after the baby's heart had already begun beating, so when a sonogram later confirmed the fetus had died, Ron and I sat stunned. In the exam room, I stared at the floor beyond my feet, and he reached for me as my silent tears dripped on my gown. During an ensuing surgery, the doctor found my pelvic area riddled with endometrial tissue, inflammatory growths that made the prospects for another pregnancy bleak. Hormone pills, artificial reproduction techniques, and visualizations of flowers blooming in my uterus didn't work. We didn't conceive again.

So the day Suz's email arrived, I confessed to her my real reason for wanting Icy. "I have empty-arms syndrome," I typed back.

I ached to swaddle babies, carry toddlers, and hug children — or, at the very least, squeeze a lovable cat.

"My dog?" Suz said. "He was an empty-arms acquisition. We got him minutes after my first in vitro fertilization failed. I had to have a baby *something*."

Suz understood. Because she was a companion of mine on the fertility journey, our conversations often revolved around ovaries and motherhood. I told her I had a feeling Ron wouldn't go for an elderly cat.

"Let's send him ESP messages," I said.

I shut my eyes and beamed him. He was in the air, thousands of miles away, on a red-eye flight to Washington, returning from a business trip.

Suz said she had an extra cat bowl and litter box I could borrow, so I made tentative plans to swing by her house on Saturday to pick up the supplies. Then I contacted Suz's vet, Dr. Whitehead, to find out more information.

"Icy will lie on your lap all day and cuddle. That's her only goal in life," Dr. Whitehead said.

What magic words. I could practically feel Icy's gentle purr and myself stroking her silky coat and kissing her between her tufted ears. I dreamed of her all night.

Ron arrived home early in the morning, bleary-eyed from the flight. First I let him sleep. Then I watched him eat. Finally, I opened my mouth.

"We're not adopting a sixteen-year-old cat," he said.

I hadn't even mentioned the peeing.

I waited a few hours before explaining the whole story again, only better this time. I added details about how Icy's ex-owners left her to be euthanized, even though she had a few good years left. And I tried to explain the hollow pang inside — a gulf that longed for a newborn baby, but one I thought could at least be tempered by a cat who wanted to do nothing but hang out and nestle all day. No dice.

Later, I tried again.

"So why don't you want to adopt Icy?"

"The logistics. What will you do with her when you're gone in February?"

"I'll take her with me."

"Be serious."

"I am serious. You're allowed to travel with a cat. I'll get one of those fashionable pet carriers — "

"The cat will go nuts."

" — and some tranquilizers."

"Who will pay for that? And who will pay for her food and litter and vet bills?"

I would if I could. When we married, Ron and I made comparable salaries. After I gave up my job as a lawyer to become a writer, my income tanked.

That evening, I schlepped down the street with a heavy heart and wandered inside the local market to buy dog food. Back home in the kitchen, I opened the bag and did a double take. I'd purchased organic cat litter.

"A sign," I said.

"Can you get a refund?" Ron asked.

I looked up at my husband and sighed. Even when he's disagreeable, he has a peaceful demeanor. He is a kind, supportive, and faithful partner. But what the hell? Couldn't he see that not only would I be rescuing Icy, but also Icy would be rescuing me? Wasn't that worth the price of a cat? Or maybe Ron was the one doing the rescuing. Maybe he was trying to save me from myself. Keeping me from setting myself up for more heartache.

The funny thing is that Ron is more of an animal lover than I am. Take spiders. I smash them with a shoe. He sets them free outside. Last Christmas he spent hours flipping through the World Wildlife Fund catalog in search of the perfect plush animal gifts (a whale for his Alaska-loving sister, a wolverine for my Michigan alum mom). Squatting close to watch a bug, I'll wait with patience as he narrates the internal thoughts of a creature looping itself around a twine of ivy ("Where am I? Lombard Street?" or "Whoa, a crumb? My lucky day!"). His old roommate in California had a cat, and although Ron tried to be sly, I noticed how, after dinner, he'd save a piece of salmon and slip it in the cat's dish. But I couldn't get him to budge about the cat I wanted. Not a bit.

I started obsessing over Icy. I kept her in my inbox. Each morning, I uploaded her picture and built our imaginary life. We lounged on my chaise with a good book, or spent the afternoon in my writing office, where I reached over from my desk to scratch her chin as she stretched out in the sunny spot by the window and yawned. We had an instant bond, as if we'd known each other for ages. True, the bond was one-sided. And I sensed a lingering awareness that it was demented to be emotionally involved with a pet I'd never met. A virtual cat. But I couldn't stop.

My preoccupation with Icy reminded me of another obsession of mine — scrolling through adoption websites in search of "special needs" kids. After selecting an exotic country, like Vietnam, I'd click through each face, wondering if I'd feel an instant connection. Before I stumbled across these Internet sites, Ron and I had started filling out adoption paperwork through a local agency. We moved smoothly through the process until I learned that international adoption is a business rife with fraudulence, abuse, and child trafficking. Ron thought we should navigate the system as best we could, certain we could find a healthy baby who needed a home. But I dragged my feet.

I found comfort in the Internet. And the more time I spent online, the more I was drawn to the special needs kids. With their physical and mental delays, these kids weren't in demand, and so they were in no danger of being caught in the web of child trafficking. At least, that was my theory. When one of the faces zapped my heart, I'd read the child's story. Fetal alcohol syndrome. HIV. Cerebral palsy. Some paragraphs were full of words that meant nothing to me but caused my pulse to race: hydrocephalus or arthrogryposis. Most special needs kids were older, and attachment disorder was practically a given. Taglines ran at the ends of their biographies: "This beautiful girl needs a family with access to the medical resources she needs," or "This spirited boy needs a family who has parented past his age." The warnings gave me pause, but I felt they were obstacles I could overcome.

I became fixated on a seven-year-old girl named Sheetal. She was from Southeast Asia and had flawless brown skin and short cropped hair. I could tell from her good-natured smile she was a happy child. Looking at her healthy glow, it was hard to believe she had a damaged liver. Her life expectancy was unknown, and her medical needs ongoing. I wanted to throw caution to the wind and take her in. As in my fantasy world with Icy, I fancied our days. I'd read books to Sheetal, and we'd walk the dog to the café, where we'd meet up with the neighborhood's newest puppies.

When Sheetal's picture disappeared from the adoption website, I suppose I shouldn't have been surprised. But I was shocked. An update said she'd found her "forever family." Part of me wanted to shout, "Wait — wrong one! Her forever family is with us." But I'd never even told Ron about her. I kept meaning to propose the idea over dinner, unsure how to bring it up.

Before long, Icy was gone, too. No one wanted to adopt her.

"My brother saw Dr. Whitehead," Suz said to me over the phone one day. "She told him she planned to put Icy down."

My heart skipped. "Planned to?"

"This was a while ago," Suz said.

At hearing the news, I wilted.

Sleeping in fits that night, I woke up with a dull ache. I felt burdened with too much loss in my life: my uprooting from California, the miscarriage three years ago, and, mixed in, the loss of what I never had: Sheetal and now Icy.

Suz emailed first thing the next morning. Icy was alive! I felt a surge inside compelling me to scoop the cat up and fold her into my arms. Dr. Whitehead had kept Icy the whole time, but Icy didn't like other cats, and Dr. Whitehead had several. Also, Dr. Whitehead was relocating to North Carolina, and when it was time for her to move, that's when Icy would be euthanized.

Unless.

That night in bed, I slid next to Ron and propped my head up on one elbow, resting my other arm on his chest. I gave one last plea for Icy. He still didn't want an old, sick cat that peed too much. I edged away and leaned back on my own pillow.

After a few moments, he held my hand. "When our lives are more suited for multiple pets, we can consider a cat," he said.

I didn't want any old cat. I wanted Icy, the *old* cat.

But why? Since the day I saw her picture, I presumed I wanted to save a cat destined to be put down. Yet it didn't make sense. Thinking over other areas of my life, I noticed I tended to shy away from commitment. I had refused to give my heart to Washington, D.C., even though we had moved from California four years earlier. I had stopped filling out the adoption paperwork halfway through the process, even though it would have put us on the path to uniting with a healthy child. I had no interest whatsoever in bringing home a young, spry kitten with an entire lifetime ahead of her. Yet I wanted Icy? And Sheetal? Why? Because they were unwanted? In desperate need of a loving home that I could unselfishly provide? I wished I were so altruistic.

But in my imagination, I *was* that person. In cyberspace, I had a big, benevolent heart. Not only could I dedicate my time and energy to mothering a cat (or a kid), I could go the distance and mother animals and children with extra needs. I could give everything I had and then some. My fantasies never included scrubbing yellow stains off the rug or sitting in a doctor's office holding the hand of a sick little girl.

Did some part of me know that neither Sheetal nor Icy would come live with us? By chasing them around — in a virtual world — was I able to hide behind their photos and avoid dealing with truth? That night, it dawned on me: Ron was the one willing to make long-term commitments. He was ready to take on the responsibilities of life's major decisions. Meanwhile, I hesitated, unsure, unstable. Always teetering on one leg, I never took a real step in any direction. And it made me wonder about all I was missing, and all I had lost.

At that moment, I made a decision. I would commit to letting go of Internet fantasies and explore why I was avoiding reality. Perhaps it was a small step, but it was an important one. Rolling closer to Ron, I tangled my arms and legs into his and rested my head on his shoulder, flesh against flesh.

19

FIRST DOG, BEST DOG

Sonia Levitin

I remember precisely the moment that our courtship changed from casual to committed. Lloyd and I were sitting on a blanket in Golden Gate Park one pleasant afternoon watching a young couple playing with their toddler and their dog, an Airedale.

I posed an important question. "Do you like dogs?"

"I love dogs," Lloyd said.

"Maybe someday," I said ingenuously, "we'll have a dog of our own."

I was eighteen, Lloyd was twenty. He obviously interpreted this as a proposal. A year later we were married, still in school, flat broke, and full of dreams. Someday we'd have a house, children, and of course a dog.

Fast-forward ten years or so. Our daughter, Shari, was three, our son, Daniel, seven. A friend informed us of a litter of German shepherds about to be born to a family living in the hills above Moraga, California, in a rustic house with quite a menagerie — some chickens, ducks, goats, and dogs. The children and I drove up to the mountain home, introduced ourselves to the family, and put in our bid for one of the puppies. We counted the days to his birth, to his weaning, to the day we would go pick him up. He was large and black and beautiful. We named him Baron.

Does memory serve me correctly? Is it true that it took only three days to housebreak Baron? Once he stole a piece of pound cake off the counter. I yelled at him, "No! Bad dog!" From then on, he understood that kitchen counters were off-limits, and that personal property must be respected. I don't recall that Baron ever stole anything else — except a volleyball that he first punctured and then refused to relinquish. At that time, he was staying with his birth family for a few days. To be fair, I must also relate that his instinct for herding caused him to mount their goat while trying to push it into a small pen, thus inflicting a wound that necessitated a visit from the vet. The entire escapade, including replacing the volleyball, set us back about eighty-four dollars. Boarding Baron would have cost a mere thirty dollars. Ever resourceful, we decided to call it a vacation, a camp/old-home-week experience for our dog, and consider it worth the cost.

Baron guarded the children. Once when the kids had disobeyed me, I stood them up against the wall in the kitchen and proceeded to deliver a stern lecture. "I'm the mother here! You do what I tell you, or else..."

Baron, about three months old, positioned himself between me and the children, confronting me with a bark and a growl.

"And that goes for you, too!" I snapped.

He meekly retreated to their side of the line, acknowledging my authority.

Baron liked to stretch out in the front hallway, guarding the door. Friends and family could enter with impunity, along with the laundry man, who arrived every Thursday morning to pick up and deliver. I left the laundry sack by the unlocked door. Baron watched the procedure, the hand coming in to pick up the sack and to deposit the package of fresh linen. "Hello there, Baron!" was the extent of conversation between them. Baron never moved, never uttered a sound. It was a marvelous example of mutual trust, with limits, of course.

Not so for the milkman, who was known as the local Lothario, operating when husbands had left for work. That man streaked from his truck to our front porch. There he dropped the milk cartons in sheer terror while Baron lunged at the door, barking hysterically. Yes, Baron was a good judge of character. Except for once, when, during an evening poker game between Lloyd and his friends, "Ted" got up to fix himself a drink and found himself pinned to the wall. Baron had his paws on Ted's shoulders and was barking ferociously into Ted's face.

It happened so fast that nobody could figure out what Ted had done to provoke Baron's reaction. The incident reinforced my conviction that animals, even near-perfect animals, can be unpredictable. On another occasion Baron did snap at our friend Mary Beth. It was July Fourth; firecrackers were bursting in neighboring yards, and Mary Beth leaned over Baron, trying to console him. He obviously held her responsible for the blasts and, while he didn't break the skin, did give her a nip on the nose. At that moment it didn't seem tactful to explain to my friend that leaning over a dog is not a good idea, especially when that dog is already tense. Even with our own beloved pets, we pause after announcing our attention, to see whether the dog is ready for love.

Looking back, I realize that each of us thought of Baron as his or her personal pet. For Lloyd and me, Baron was the perfect hiking companion. He loved wandering in the hills near our house and trekking through old western towns on Sunday outings. He was always the first one in the car, after dutifully emptying his bladder before every trip. I had taught him to respond to the command "bathroom," a device that has benefited all of my family's people-dog relationships ever since.

Baron wasn't a particularly sociable animal. He had few friends among the neighborhood dogs. Once the children gave him a doggie birthday party with a hamburger cake. It was touch and go. The animals just wanted to eat and leave. Forget party games. What Baron loved were balls, any type, anywhere. He ferreted them out of the thorniest thickets, grabbed them rolling along the gutter, snapped them up in midair. Once, at the Historical Society picnic, he caught a fly ball sailing toward first base. We thought it was great, but he was not invited to the next ball game.

What Baron liked best was a good one-on-one relationship, as when Dan whispered secrets into his ear or Shari
read him a poem she had just written.

Baron had only two canine friends ever. The first was
Squaw, a black Lab who lived in the cul-de-sac behind
ours. When Squaw was in heat, Baron decided to claim the
prerogative of a long-standing friendship, and he eagerly
mounted her. She rebuffed him with a snap and a growl.
Baron's pride prevented him from ever attempting another
mating.

New neighbors moved in next door with a very small
dachshund named Floyd. Her owners only laughed when
we pointed out the incongruity of the name for a dog that
came into heat so often we were convinced it was part rabbit.
Baron would sit at the window wailing, howling, and moan-
ing. He was obviously in love with Floyd and frustrated. We
attempted all sorts of remedies, from barricades to medica-
tions. At last we reached into our pockets and paid to have
the dachshund spayed.

Years passed. We moved to Southern California. Our
new home had an atrium bounded by a fancy iron gate. We
didn't need a doorbell, as this immediately became Baron's
domain. Barks, echoes, and shouts announced every arrival
and made us unpopular with the neighbors. I rationalized
that it was better to discourage drop-in visitors, salespeople,
and deliveries so that I could focus on my writing. With
Baron at the gate, our home was something of a fortress —
not serene, but certainly secure.

As Baron began to age, we decided to get a puppy.
How could we endure the inevitable loss of our friend but

by dividing our attention and eventually coming to love another dog? We decided that Baron should become a father, and we searched for a likely match. It had to be a German shepherd, of course, good tempered, smart, and beautiful. Alas, when I apprised the vet of our plan, he informed me that ten-year-old dogs are usually infertile or impotent. We kept this shocking news from Baron and proceeded to look around for a perfect puppy. We looked for a puppy exactly like Baron. But dogs, like people, are individuals. Each has a unique personality and set of desires and faults.

Having heard of a fine kennel in a town some sixty miles away, we took off one day to investigate and returned home with a long-haired German shepherd pup that on the way home we named Barney.

That first afternoon Barney began eating the sofa in my study. He urinated on Lloyd's new loafers. (I tried to assure Lloyd that this was just a sign of submission, proclaiming Lloyd as the alpha male. He wasn't impressed.) That first day, Barney took a flying leap right through the open slats in our staircase and fell down an entire flight, landing in a heap on the bottom. Later we thought maybe he'd become befuddled from the fall, because he proved to be the most exasperating, difficult, untrainable dog we ever had.

Barney had a fetish for rocks and fossilized bones, which he dug up from the yard and dumped onto the deck, making a terrible racket. He attacked the garden hoses, tried to swim in his water dish, and dug out the roses. He leapt onto my head and clung there while I was driving. Barney never guarded anything. He was terrified of intruders, trees, other dogs, and squirrels. I took him to puppy class. The teacher said he was "an introvert" who refused to join the circle and heel. He caused me much embarrassment, escaping from the class with me racing after him. The teacher used him as an example of a "thoroughly undersocialized animal." He was the only one who did not graduate. It was a humbling experience.

As for Barney's relationship with Baron, it was always somewhat dicey. Baron remained the king, top dog, and protector. That first night when we took them for a walk together, some noise sent Barney into a panic. Without missing a beat, Barney planted himself directly underneath Baron, and both continued to race along the street like some new eight-legged creature.

Baron ignored Barney's attempts to cuddle and converse; he merely tolerated the puppy. As a result, I revised my thinking for future reference: after this I would always have two dogs fairly close in age, so that they could be real playmates and enjoy their golden years together.

Barney never really outgrew his aggravating habits. However, he did vindicate himself by rescuing two kittens on the very day of their birth. Apparently some stray dropped them in our yard. Barney (maybe thinking they were fossilized bones) brought them carefully up onto our deck. I thought they were dead rats until investigation and a plaintive "meow" proved they were kittens needing a home, around-the-clock feeding, and tender care. For a mom with a nearly empty nest, it was no contest. We ended up being the parents of Jinxie and Jessie, along with Barney and Baron.

Meanwhile, Baron continued to age rapidly and pathetically. The vet gave him six months to a year, maybe. When

Baron had an encounter with a skunk one night, it took him three days to recover, and he was never quite the same afterward. He could no longer navigate the stairs, so he made his home in the atrium, lying on a thick lounge pad, still attempting to guard the gate. His coat lost its luster. His face was pinched and lean. The sheet that covered his pad was often smeared with blood, for he developed sores on his elbows that became ulcerated. Arthritis had settled in his joints. It hurt him to stand, lie down, and walk. No longer could he use his forepaws independently. He barely made it to the vacant lot next door to relieve himself. Sometimes he fell.

The question burned in my mind. What should we do? How long should we avoid deciding and watch the slow, agonizing process of deterioration? With death the inevitable end, must we wait until he had pain past bearing?

But did we have the right to judge life's rightful length or its quality? What made me the guardian of the fate of another creature, one who couldn't communicate his thoughts on the matter?

At Thanksgiving, when Dan came home from college, he was shocked at Baron's decline. He reproached us. "Can't you see he's suffering? How can you let him live this way?"

We talked about it, hoping the problem would resolve itself and Baron would die gently in his sleep. As December came and the weather grew cold, I knew I had to act. We decided that the vet would come to the house the following day and administer the shot that would end Baron's life. I wanted him to die at home, with us. Shari and I would be together for his last moments. The ASPCA would arrive precisely on time, to take away his body.

That night we took Baron for his last walk. It was crisp and cold and the moon was nearly round, like a big silver plate, seen between the leaves of our neighbor's gigantic eucalyptus tree. I wanted to show him the moon, but he kept his head down. Baron plodded along, unaware that this was a special moment, a last time. I stopped to pet him, to feel his rough coat and the knotty bones on his back. I wanted to convey by my touch how much I loved him. He sat down and scratched his ear, his hind paw thumping on the sidewalk. I almost laughed at the incongruity: the sentimental person, the practical dog. I think Baron would have said we were doing the right thing.

Since Baron and Barney, we have had other dogs, some "on loan" when our children were in new jobs or new relationships. Of course the temporary became permanent, and we liked it that way. We fostered Charlotte and Isabella, our children's dogs. Charlotte was undoubtedly the cleverest of the lot, finding her way home from two miles away in a rainstorm. Isabella was learning how to read, using uniform blocks with words stenciled on them. Dan, now a scientist, had begun this training, and I agreed to continue it. (I didn't tell Dan, but it never really worked.) Sometimes I go through my photographs heaped in various boxes. Most are pictures of our dogs. Barney, who after many years drowned in our pool. (Dan insisted that incontinence had led him to commit suicide.) There was Bridget, a German shepherd so beautiful that her birth family called her "Pretty Face." Bruno, our last shepherd, was so unruly that we took him to a dog whisperer, who suggested we send him to the army. We didn't. Then came Kinia, a Rhodesian Ridgeback. To this day I'll stop any owner of a Ridgeback to tell about my Kinia's intelligence, loyalty, and yes, sense of humor. Now we have Buddy and Shadow, two midsize black rescue dogs of uncertain parentage. They are less robust than the large breeds we used to favor, but then, so are we. We talk about our dogs as if they were our children. And in a way, of course, they are. They are part of our family lore, our laughter, and our learning.

We loved them all, but there is something about the first dog we shared as a family that was different. Whenever we reminisce about our dogs, as often we do, when we mention Baron we share a certain look, a special smile, and we conclude, "Baron was the best dog."

20

TAKING STOCK

Thomas McGuane

The enchantment of riding is a mysterious thing that generates never-ending reflection for those who wish to understand the mild euphoria produced by the proximity of horses. This is not the province of equestrian recreationists alone; the evidence abounds that Native Americans, cavalrymen, cowboys, and farmers were vulnerable to this sweeping affection, which finds itself in close bonds on the one hand and insatiable accumulation on the other. Among the accumulators are buffalo-hunting Indians, Coca-Cola heirs, sheiks, oilmen, and soon-to-be-bankrupt professors. The Plains Indians were liberated from the midwestern forests by the horse, and the cruelest strikes against their civilization were the execution of their horses, as at the Sand Creek Massacre, where a Methodist minister named Carrington tried to put a whole people afoot by killing their mounts.

That my house adjoins my corrals is one of the blessings of my adult life. I start very few days without taking my
coffee out to stand among our horses so that we may contemplate the beginning of another day. When I'm stressful
or troubled that I can't make a piece of work come out right,
or a friend or family member has received unsettling health
news, or some other unhappy or unpleasant feeling comes
over me that won't find a quiet place of storage, a visit to the
horses nearly always produces relief. Relief and perspective,
which is perhaps the same thing.

When we had an irrevocably dying horse, my veterinarian told me that we had to change our perspective and try to
understand that animals accept what happens to them. And
it's not as if they don't know. They know. We humans, on
the other hand, have evolved to accept nothing. We don't accept how fast we go, how long we live, how much we eat,
how frequently we copulate. Our position is: *It's all negotia-
ble* or *I'll buy my way out of this.* In the life of horses, grave
things happen from birth to death and they never negotiate;
their bank accounts contain only the memories of their race.

Back to my corrals: The gates to native grass pastures
are seldom closed, but there they are to see us anyway.
We've swindled them with treats but are flattered because
they seem glad to see us, and affection must be dealt even-
handedly to avoid jealousy. The personalities are very distinct: the erratic yearlings striving, not always successfully,
for acceptance; the old mare with the frozen ears who requires twice the space the others need; a daydreaming
mother-to-be, the star cutting horse who declared at twelve,
by refusing ever to get into a trailer again, that her days of

competition were over; the foursquare and uncomplicat-
edly heroic cow horse who shambles around like Ollie the
Dragon but breathes fire when working cattle; my wife's
cutting horse, informal inspector of all ranch activities; my
head-case saddle horse, who spooks at grasshoppers; the
trusting young mare who among all our horses is alone allowed to transport the grandchildren; the tall bay mare, the
stately mother of champions — and I'm afraid what some
would say are too many others. The largest group is the pen-
sioners, aged ranch horses living serenely in a riparian cot-
tonwood forest; and, beyond, the burial ground where our
old mounts, old friends, lie — most at the end of long lives
but some that were too short: a fall that broke a neck, a light-
ning strike, a twisted gut.

In 1957, I loped across a Wyoming pasture trying to rope
a calf. After three unsuccessful throws, my horse stopped
suddenly on his front feet and I sailed onto the ground in
front of him, useless lariat in hand. To this day, I remember
the contemplative look on that horse's face as he gazed at me
on the ground, and the quiet acceptance as he let me climb
on again. We'd agreed to accept my limitations, and to jog
on home together. It's unique to share a time, to share a job,
with a partner who doesn't judge you, even over the span of
years. It occurs to you that you might do the same. Long ex-
posure to horses should teach tolerance. One accomplished
equestrian said you'll never be a champion until you understand and accept the limitations of each horse. Certainly
horses accept that humans can't see very far, smell very
much, or hear very well. Our lurching two-legged slow-
ness must seem amusing to any horse that doesn't wish to

be caught. Every day, a rider must be reminded by his horse how little he notices about the surface of the earth. Squirrelly as we are, horses tolerate us and our addled, sex-crazed, money grubbing, vengeful brains.

Apparently there are more and more horses, more than ever before, shaded up, switching flies, traveling in single file to water, bucking off cowboys, leading parades, amusing children, skidding logs, sorting cattle, climbing mountains, carrying supplies — another society, almost, invading human loneliness.

21

DOG YEARS

Mark Doty

First, he falls on a few stairs on the way down to the street, missing his footing. The lightbulb's burnt out on the landing, and he seems furious about it, trying to find the step; perhaps, to his dimmed eyes, that dim hallway's really just darkness. Then, a few days later, even with new bulbs illuminating the way, he stumbles going up, and actually tumbles down nearly a whole flight to the landing, scaring Paul half to death. Happily, Arden seems partly made of rubber, his limbs twisting akimbo without any apparent harm. But the day comes when the stairs to the apartment are impossible; that old right hind leg just seems a delicate, withering thing, and there's simply no way he can manage. We carry him, but it's ridiculous to try to lug him up and down every time he needs to go out, even when I remember to keep my knees bent. And it's doubtless awful for him, one of us trying to lug seventy-five pounds of dog up and down the stairs every time he needs to go out. He *does* feel light now, in the way that old men get stringier and less meaty, but there's still a lot of him.

Luckily, it's a semester when we're off work, more or less. We have freedom to move, and can take Arden up to the house in Provincetown much earlier than we'd usually go to our summer place. We arrive in April, when it's leaden and chill, and the house seems glad to see us, suddenly lit with lamps and fires and habitation. To be there is a huge, immediate relief: Arden can live on one floor and spend as much time outside as he likes. We don't have to worry about getting him quickly in and out, and if he doesn't make it outside one day, it's not a problem — these old wood floors have already seen two hundred years of action, and nothing's going to hurt them. Plus he's known this house forever. It's a fine, easy place to be old.

And, so, six weeks pass, as the calendar moves toward Arden's sixteenth birthday, sometime in April, then on into May.

DR. KAISER IS GENTLE WITH ARDEN, and wouldn't dream of doing anything invasive. I like him; he's soft-spoken, curious about the creature before him. Though he is physically large, he does not seem to think of himself as such — the way Newfoundlands, say, seem vaguely apologetic for their size, a bit of slow delicacy in their largeness. Dr. Kaiser thinks it's great that Arden's had such a long span on earth, and he knows how attached to him we are. He makes no unrealistic attempts or promises or offers at all. Now it's all about comfort; he understands that, at this point, whatever life is left to this old survivor is, as they say, gravy.

Arden, naturally, does not like Dr. Kaiser as much as I do. He puts up with him, though, and cautiously accepts the liver-flavored vitamins the vet holds out to him.

Now the nickname that Paul has always favored for Arden seems the best: Tiny. Brave fellow, huffing along, figuring out how to move that uncooperative body from spot to spot. "Where is that Tiny," we say. Napping under the budding forsythia, out on the gravel staring at sparrows. Although we sleep upstairs, Arden soon abandons any notion of coming up with us: he's happy to stay downstairs on the living-room rug, or, if we've built a fire that evening, on the bare floor of the dining room, where it's cooler. As spring comes on, he's more and more in the garden, staying in one place for long stretches. We have some little outings: trips to the vet, followed by a drive to the beach. The last time we go, he's clearly too sore and tired to even get out of the car, but we leave the tailgate open so he can look out and breathe in that current of Atlantic air.

And then he's in the kitchen all the time, where his food and water are, on the cool quarry-tile floor. People always said to me, *You'll know when it's time*, and I never believed it — not with this dog, who wanted so much to stay in the world. I was terrified that his body would fail him, would refuse to go another step, an awful sprawl beneath him, and he'd be looking at me in a confusion and panic, just wanting to live.

Dr. Kaiser says, "Call me any time, I'll come to the house. You'll know when it's time."

Arden seems nervous, his breathing's hard. In pain, I think. The Triumph goes unfinished. He falls, and I try to reach beneath him and lift up those crumpled hindquarters, and he cries out terribly.

There's a Friday morning when I wake up and hear him crying before I've even walked into the kitchen, and there he is, sprawled on the floor in a puddle of urine and feces he's been trying to drag himself out of, completely helpless. And the look on his face — well, I know what it means, beyond any doubt.

I clean him up and call Dr. Kaiser, who understands the situation but can't come till Sunday. Certainly, it's better for us that we have a little time. I think it'll be all right; we can take care of him. What I'd imagined I wouldn't be able to stand was the feeling that Arden would still want to live, that he'd have every intention of going on no matter how helpless his body: hell on earth. But that isn't the case; what was entirely plain to me in his face that morning was that he was through, that he'd welcome an exit.

Once I've made the call, Arden seems to lighten, to change, as if he knows the path is clear. He still can't move, but he seems at ease, distraction giving way to that old, clear gaze, his tension evaporating. It's as if there's an element of relief for Paul and me, what we've so long known was coming is here at last, and Arden must feel it, too.

And now we give him the warmest and lightest weekend we can. He seems to relax utterly. We spend time brushing and stroking him. We cuddle him up and talk. He sleeps in the garden, his last night, in the cool air under the stars, and Sunday morning has grilled chicken for breakfast, and he's sprawled sleepily on the gravel by the gate when Dr. Kaiser comes. My sense, for whatever it's worth, is that he knows perfectly well where we've arrived. Does he give one little growl at the vet, as if for old times' sake? As if it were his duty, and he'd be some other dog if he didn't?

This is unmitigatedly awful and not so at all; I remind myself this is exactly what I'd want, for someone to love me enough not to allow me to live in pain when I don't want to; that it's part of our work — this is what Dr. Kaiser has said to us — part of our stewardship, seeing Arden out of the world.

I have my face down against that smooth muzzle, the ears that still smell, as they have all his life, of corn muffins. Paul's holding him from the other side, so that we can both be in his gaze. We each speak to him quietly. First, there's a shot to relax him, to make sure the second shot will work, and I don't think he even feels it. And then we ease him out of that worn-out body with a kiss, and he's gone like a whisper, the easiest breath.

WE'D LONG PLANNED TO BURY HIM IN THE GARDEN, near where Beau lies, in his favorite spot under the forsythia. But when it came to it, truly we couldn't do it. Wasn't Arden a dog who always really just wanted to be with us anyway? Leave it to Beau for commingling with all things wild; Arden preferred his human company. So, we let the vet take his body to be cremated, down Cape someplace, his ashes to be returned in a few days. Dr. Kaiser lifts him — still a serious bulk, though he looks so light now — and then, oh! what empties out my heart all over again, how his neck lolls like a loose flower on a stem. Just like Wally's; how, after months and months of rigidity, the gradual paralysis afflicting his nervous system and muscles and pulling his head tightly to one side — and then, suddenly, in death, that tightness released as if it had never been there. Who knew that Arden had been holding his neck with all that tension? He'd worked so hard, old soldier, to hold himself upright, to will his uncooperating hips to the next step, the next position. I'm remembering the tension in his shoulders, the way those muscles worked overtime, to compensate. And now, all effort released, the neck just floats.

The vet sets his sweet body in the back of the black pickup truck. I can't help it, I have to rearrange his head and neck so he looks comfortable, even though I know it's absurd. The vet understands my gesture, and we thank him for all he's done for us, and then he drives away.

WE TRY OUR BEST. *A good end*, we tell ourselves, *a fine end, the best we could do.* We talk about Mr. Arden and the stories of his days, and then we don't, for a while, and we each allow ourselves to weep — usually one at a time, because somehow doing it together just seems too much for us to take. *A long life*, we say, *a fine life, and not nearly enough.*

Sometimes the house is so empty we can hardly bear it, and then sometimes it seems like no one's gone — isn't Arden in one of his favored spots, watching us? Won't he, in a moment, come around the door? He's an absence and a presence both — the way he will be, to a greater or lesser degree, for years to come.

We keep collecting his hair in its little dark puffs from the floor.

Paul finds an empty can of Triumph in the recycling bin, and we put the hair in there, on the mantel.

We make a memorial ad, as people in our small town like to do, to tell the community about the passing of loved dogs, and take it down to the newspaper office. The fellow who takes our ad has an old dog, too. We bring a photo of Arden on the beach, and his name and dates, and a stanza from the most unabashed elegy for a dog I know, Robinson Jeffers's "The Housedog's Grave," in which an English bulldog named Haig speaks from his grave, outside the window of the house where he'd lived:

> *I've changed my ways a little, I cannot now*
> *Run with you in the evenings along the shore,*
> *Except in a kind of dream, and you, if you dream a moment,*
> *You see me there.*

Wouldn't you know that the most misanthropic of poets would write the warmest of elegies for his dog? I email the poem to people who've known Arden, to tell them he's gone. I cut out the last words, and put them on the table where I write, next to a photograph of Arden in the deep green of the summer garden: *I am not lonely. I am not afraid. I am still yours.*

They help a bit, those lines.

Paul and I are strangely unanchored. We take ourselves out for strolls to the bay, go across town to look at the marsh, amble back, noticing the gardens and the new shops. We stop for coffee. We sit a long time, on the bench in front of the coffee bar. No hurry. This feels strange to me, unfamiliar. For sixteen years, there has been someone at home, waiting to go for a walk.

EPILOGUE

My cat Stuart with the failing kidneys had to be put to sleep while I was working on this book. In the past it always seemed that my animals died suddenly with no forewarning — in accidents, or in emergency races to the vet where they were put to sleep quickly to end their pain; there was never any planning to it. But last December I spent a day knowing that Stuart's hours were numbered: his veterinarian, Bob Goldman, was coming to the house that evening to put him to sleep. I had no options — he had stopped eating, wouldn't drink water, and this most meticulous of cats had begun to wet his bed. He was peeing blood.

To have the end of Stuart's life scheduled was a huge blessing of course — a compassionate, skilled doctor was coming to our house to ease Stuart out of pain in his own little bed right next to my computer, in the company of people who loved him, as well as of his sister, Charlotte — a cat who might not have exactly loved him but was his flesh and blood after all. (I have to admit that Stuart had a long history of being abusive to his sister, beating her up on occasion and trying to ignore her the rest of the time. They were never friends, never groomed one another or curled up together.)

In spite of how sick he was the final day, Stuart, ever the bon vivant, made trips down to the kitchen and out into the courtyard. This caused me to second-guess myself. He looked so beautiful! How could a creature still so gorgeous be dying? I cried, wrote in my journal, drank ginger tea, Googled end-of-life issues for cats on the Internet, and emailed back and forth with the vet.

Had I planned an execution? That's how it felt. I didn't want to endure this huge wave of grief bearing down on me. I got angry. Wait a minute: My cat is just going to disappear? Be *gone*? This warm, sweet body next to my computer will *vanish*? How can you wrap your mind around something like this?

It was raining outside, but then it cleared to a magnificent sunset. Which made everything worse. *Give me a sign*, I begged Stuart. I realized I was waiting for him to be almost dead before the vet came, but he didn't look almost dead. Did I have the right to play God? And then suddenly Stuart lowered himself down on my computer and made a sound I'd never heard him make before — half groan, half growl. An exhausted, end-of-the-road sound, loud and final.

CLASSICAL MUSIC PLAYED, and the lights in my office were dim, when Bob Goldman arrived at seven that night. He petted Stuart and talked to him for a while, then gave him a sedative to relax him. With the music playing, the soft lighting, all of us petting Stuart and whispering to him, the feeling in the room was calm and sweet, like some kind of low-key celebration or church service. Bob gave Stuart another shot and he began to sleep soundly, but his strong heart kept beating. It was almost an hour before Stuart was finally gone — peaceful in his bed on my desk, and astonishingly, his sister, who had watched the events of the past hour, was curled up next to him.

AND NOW FIVE MONTHS LATER, Charlotte is living out her final days. I know it's close to the end; she eats very little and no longer leaves my office. But she seems peaceful and content, spoiled with small bites of baby food and constant attention, exuding a patience and dignity that you never see in younger cats, no matter how adorable they are. And I think: maybe death is not so fearful a thing. Is this what we can learn from our animals when they navigate their passage out of this world with such acceptance and grace?

When I pet Charlotte, her fur feels warm from the sun pouring in the window and she smells of baby food. She purrs.

CONTRIBUTORS

CECILIA MANGUERRA BRAINARD is the author of seven books, including the novels *Magdalena* and *When the Rainbow Goddess Wept*. She is the recipient of several awards, including a California Arts Council Fellowship in Fiction, and teaches creative writing at the UCLA Extension Writers' Program. Cecilia managed her cat's Facebook account (Kiki D'Rose), which was linked from her blog, Cbrainard .blogspot.com.

MAY-LEE CHAI is the author of seven books, including her award-winning memoir, *Hapa Girl*, and most recently the novel *Dragon Chica*. She is the recipient of an NEA Grant, a Literature Fellowship in Prose. Her short stories and essays have been published in.the United States and abroad, including in *Seventeen*, *Missouri Review*, *North American Review*, and the *Jakarta Post Weekender* magazine.

MICHAEL CHITWOOD's poetry and fiction have appeared in the *Atlantic Monthly*, *Poetry*, the *New Republic*, *Virginia Quarterly Review*, and numerous other journals. He has published six books of poems, including *Gospel Road Going* and *Spill*, both of which were awarded the Roanoke-Chowan Award for Poetry. He has also published collections of essays and short stories. His latest book is *Poor-Mouth Jubilee*, published by Tupelo Press in 2010. He teaches at the University of North Carolina at Chapel Hill.

MELISSA CISTARO's personal essays have been published in the *New Ohio Review* and online at Anderbo.com. She lives in Northern California with her husband and three children and has recently completed her first novel.

MARK DOTY has published eight volumes of poetry, and won the National Book Award for Poetry in 2008 for *Fire to Fire: New and Selected Poems*. He's the author of four volumes of nonfiction, including *Dog Years*, which was a *New York Times* bestseller in 2007. He teaches at Rutgers University.

SAMANTHA DUNN is the author of the novel *Failing Paris* and the memoirs *Not By Accident* and *Faith in Carlos Gomez*. She is also coeditor of the short-story anthology *Women on the Edge: Writing from Los Angeles*. A contributing editor at the *Los Angeles Times Magazine*, she has had her work featured in *O: The Oprah Magazine*, *Ms.*, *Redbook*, and many other national magazines. She is married and has a son.

LINZI GLASS's first novel, *The Year the Gypsies Came*, was published in six languages and voted one of the best books for young adults by the American Library Association. Her third book, and latest novel, *Finding Danny*, combines her two passions, writing and animal rescue. She teaches writing through the UCLA Extension Writers' Program and is the executive director and cofounder of the Forgotten Dog Foundation, a nonprofit organization dedicated to rescuing, rehabilitating, and re-homing dogs in need.

ROBERT GOLDMAN practices veterinary medicine in Mar Vista, California. He is past president of the Southern California Veterinary Medical Association, and is the former chief of staff of the Los Angeles Spaymobile.

MONICA HOLLOWAY is the author of two memoirs, *Driving With Dead People* (a *Newsweek* Best Book pick), and the bestselling story of her son, Wills, and his beloved dog, *Cowboy & Wills*. Her essay "Red Boots and Cole Haans" appeared in the anthology *Mommy Wars*, and her articles have been published in national magazines. Monica lives in Los Angeles with her family and thirteen animals, eight of which are hermit crabs.

TED KOOSER served two terms as U.S. Poet Laureate and, during his first term, was awarded the Pulitzer Prize for Poetry. He says it's all downhill from there.

ANNE LAMOTT is the author of six novels as well as four best-selling books of nonfiction, including *Operating Instructions* and *Bird by Bird: Some Instructions on Writing and Life*. She has won a Guggenheim Fellowship, and her biweekly *Salon* magazine "online diary," *Word by Word*, was voted the Best of the Web by *Time* magazine. Her latest novel, *Imperfect Birds*, was published in 2010.

SONIA LEVITIN has written over forty books in various genres, both for children and adults. Her most recent project is a stage musical, *Return*, based on her award-winning novel *The Return*. She lives in Southern California with her husband, Lloyd, a professor at the University of Southern California, and two rescue dogs, Buddy, a Lab mix, and Shadow, a chow chow mix. Sonia has taught the craft of writing at UCLA Extension for many years. Her website is SoniaLevitin.com.

THOMAS MCGUANE is the author of ten novels, three works of nonfiction, and two collections of stories, including *Driving on the Rim*. He lives on a ranch in McLeod, Montana.

BILLY MERNIT, author of *Imagine Me and You: A Novel* (Random House/Shaye Areheart), began his writing career as a composer-lyricist; his songs have been recorded by Carly Simon and Judy Collins. He's since written for television (NBC's *Santa Barbara*), and while working as both screenwriter and script consultant, he has become known as "the guru of rom-com" for his bestselling screenwriting textbook, *Writing the Romantic Comedy* (HarperCollins).

JUDITH LEWIS MERNIT spent sixteen years at the *LA Weekly*, where she wrote about the arts, technology, and the environment. Her work has appeared in *Mother Jones*, *Wired*, *Sierra*, and *High Country News*, where she is currently a contributing editor. She has won awards from the Los Angeles Press Club, the Association of Alternative Newsweeklies, and the Dog Writers Association of America. She lives in Venice, California, with her husband, two dogs, and two cats.

JOE MORGENSTERN is the film critic of the *Wall Street Journal* and won the 2005 Pulitzer Prize for Criticism. He was a foreign correspondent for the *New York Times*, theater and movie critic for the *New York Herald Tribune*, movie critic for *Newsweek*, and a columnist for the *Los Angeles Herald Examiner*. His magazine journalism includes articles for the *New Yorker*, the *New York Times Magazine*, *Playboy*, and the *Columbia Journalism Review*. He has written television scripts, including *The Boy in the Plastic Bubble* and several episodes of *Law & Order*.

ROBIN ROMM is the author of a collection of stories, *The Mother Garden*, which was a finalist for a PEN USA award, and a memoir, *The Mercy Papers*, which was a *New York Times* Notable Book of the Year, an *Entertainment Weekly* Top Five Nonfiction Book of the Year, and a *San Francisco Chronicle* Best Book of the Year. Her writing has appeared in many publications, such as the *New York Times*, the *U.K. Observer*, the *San Francisco Chronicle*, *Tin House*, and the *Threepenny Review*.

JENNY ROUGH has written essays and articles for the *Washington Post*, *Los Angeles Times*, *Yoga Journal*, *More*, *USA Weekend*, and *Writer's Digest*, among other publications. With roots in both coasts, she's a regular contributor to

Whole Life Times and is the Green Scene columnist for the *Washington Examiner* in D.C. Her essays have also appeared as commentaries on public radio. Her website is Jenny Rough.com.

CAROLYN SEE is the author of five novels, including *The Handyman* and *Golden Days*. She is also the author of *Dreaming: Hard Luck and Good Times in America*. She is a book reviewer for the *Washington Post* and is on the board of PEN Center USA West. She has a PhD in American literature from UCLA, where she is an adjunct professor of English. Her awards include the Robert Kirsch Body of Work Award (1993) and a Guggenheim Fellowship in fiction. She lives in California.

JANE SMILEY is the author of many books and essays and won a Pulitzer Prize for her novel *A Thousand Acres*. Her latest projects are a novel for adults, *Private Life*, and a series of horse books for young readers. The first of these, *The Georges and the Jewels*, was published in fall 2009; the second, *A Good Horse*, in fall 2010; and the third, *True Blue*, is due out in fall 2011. Jane Smiley has six horses and three dogs and lives in California.

JACQUELINE WINSPEAR, originally from the United Kingdom, has lived in California since 1990. She has written articles and essays for a range of magazines and for radio, and is also the author of the award-winning and *New York Times–*bestselling series featuring psychologist and investigator Maisie Dobbs. When not writing, Jackie spends as much time as she can with her two beloved horses, Sara, a Dutch Warmblood, and Oliver, a Friesian; or hiking with her rescued black Lab, Maya (aka Mayakin, Mayabelle, Mayaboo, Boo…).

VICTORIA ZACKHEIM is the author of the novel *The Bone Weaver* and creator, contributing author, and/or editor of four anthologies: *The Face in the Mirror*; *For Keeps*; *The Other Woman*; and *He Said What?* (Seal/Perseus, 2011). She writes for On the Road Productions, teaches personal-essay writing in the UCLA Extension Writers' Program, and writes and records commentaries and book reviews for the talk radio program *The Mimi Geerges Show*. She lives in San Francisco. Her website is VictoriaZackheim.com.

ACKNOWLEDGMENTS

There would be no book without the contributors, and I'm so deeply grateful for all their essays. Thank you, *Cherished* writers (and you *are* cherished): Cecilia Brainard, May-lee Chai, Michael Chitwood, Melissa Cistaro, Mark Doty, Samantha Dunn, Linzi Glass, Monica Holloway, Anne Lamott, Sonia Levitin, Thomas McGuane, Billy Mernit, Judith Lewis Mernit, Joe Morgenstern, Robin Romm, Jenny Rough, Carolyn See, Jane Smiley, Jacqueline Winspear, and Victoria Zackheim (who also introduced me to the world of editing anthologies). And thank you, Ted Kooser, for the perfect poem for this anthology.

Nor would there be a book without Dr. Robert Goldman — friend, student, and veterinarian to my animals — who gave me the idea for this anthology. Thank you, dear friend, for not only the idea but also for the loving care of Stuart and Charlotte.

Once again and always, thanks to my agent, Lisa Erbach Vance, for her amazing energy, loyalty, smarts, and priceless advice.

And to Sally Court for always knowing what's needed and what is not.

Thanks to my stepdaughter, Leslie Adams; Gene Collins; and my Montana girlfriends, for teaching me what I know about riding horses.

And cheers to Rob Daly, who solves all my Mac problems.

A profound thank you to my editor, Jason Gardner, and the whole gang at New World Library, especially copyeditor Bonnie Hurd, Kristen Cashman, Tona Pearce Myers, Tracy Cunningham, Munro Magruder, Monique Muhlenkamp, and Kim Corbin. You all are a joy to work with.

And to my daughters, who are part of the stories, especially Gillan, who turns her love of animals into action; to my husband, who is allergic to cats but lived in the same house with Stuart and Charlotte for thirteen years; and to all my grandchildren — Emma, Axel, Grace, Cara, William, Vincent, and Josiah — who carry on the love of animals.

PERMISSIONS

The editor and publisher wish to thank the following publishers, authors, and publications:

Carnegie Mellon University Press for permission to reprint "January 19" by Ted Kooser from *Winter Morning Walks: One Hundred Postcards to Jim Harrison*. Copyright 2000 by Ted Kooser.

Michael Chitwood for "The General," originally published in *The Sun* magazine, June 2004. Reprinted with permission from the author.

Jane Smiley for "Mr. T.'s Heart," originally published in *Practical Horseman*. Copyright 1999 by Jane Smiley/Horse Heaven. Reprinted with permission from the Aaron M. Priest Literary Agency and The Friedrich Agency.

Riverhead Books, an imprint of Penguin Group (USA), for permission to reprint "This Dog's Life" from *Plan B:*

ABOUT THE EDITOR

Barbara Abercrombie has published novels and nonfiction for adults and picture books for children, including the award-winning *Charlie Anderson*. Her essays and articles have appeared in national publications as well as in many anthologies. Her most recent book is *Courage & Craft: Writing Your Life into Story*. She teaches creative writing at UCLA Extension and lives in Santa Monica, California, and Twin Bridges, Montana, with her husband and rescue dog, Nelson.

All royalties from this book will be donated to
Best Friends Animal Society.